Yasuhisa Kohyama

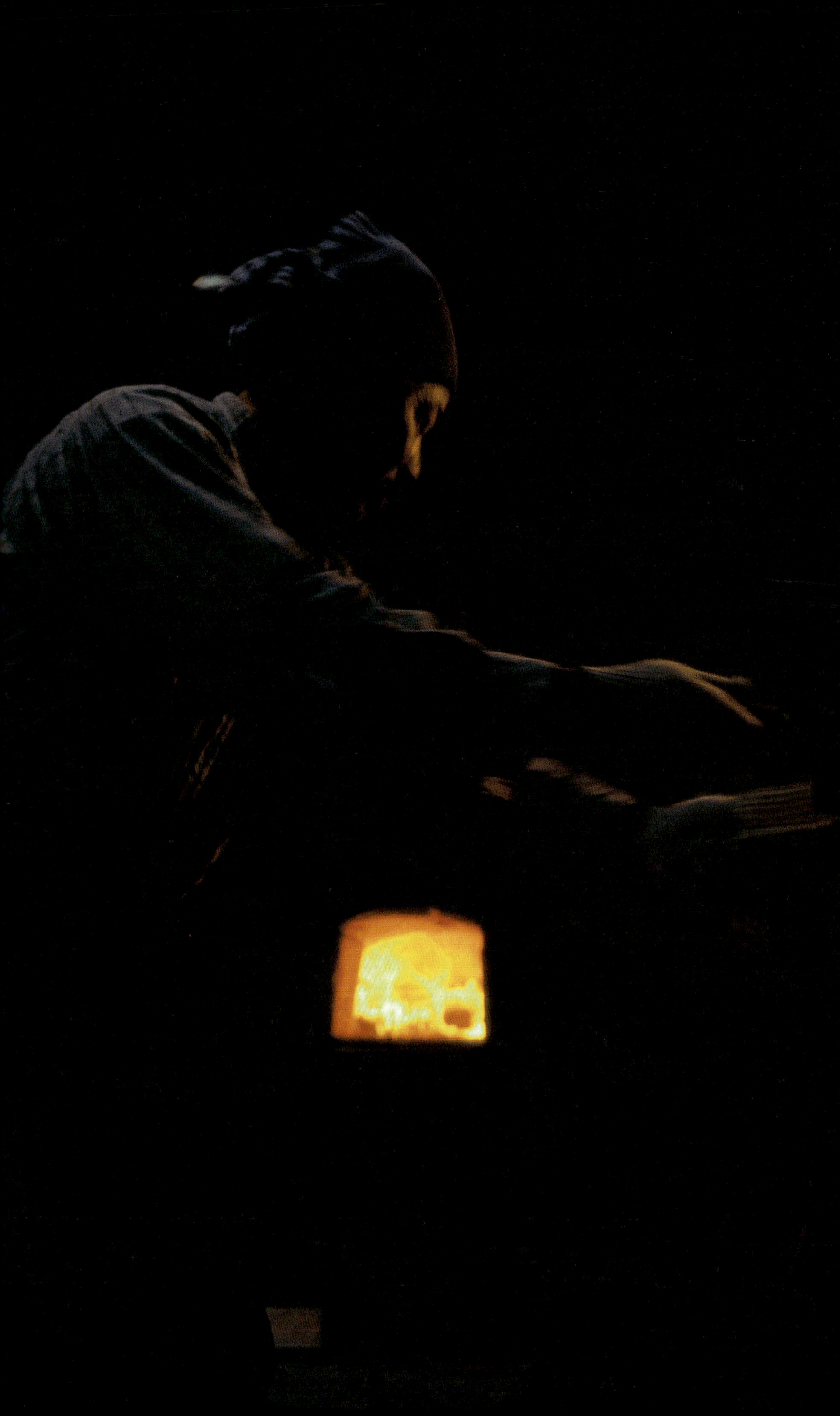

Yasuhisa Kohyama

The Art of Ceramics

TEXTS BY

Susan Jefferies
Michael R. Cunningham
Yoshiaki Inui
Jack Lenor Larsen

ARNOLDSCHE ART PUBLISHERS

AUTHORS
Susan Jefferies
Michael R. Cunningham
Yoshiaki Inui
Jack Lenor Larsen

TEXT EDITING
Wendy Brouwer, Stuttgart

ARNOLDSCHE PROJECT COORDINATION
Dirk Allgaier, Marion Boschka

LAYOUT
Karina Moschke, Stuttgart

OFFSET REPRODUCTIONS
Repromayer, Reutlingen

PRINTED BY
Gorenjski tisk storitve, Kranj

PAPER
Profibulk 150 g/sqm

BIBLIOGRAPHIC INFORMATION PUBLISHED BY
THE DEUTSCHE NATIONALBIBLIOTHEK
The Deutsche Nationalbibliothek lists this publication in the Deutsche Nationalbibliografie; detailed bibliographic data are available in the Internet at www.d-nb.de.

ISBN 978-3-89790-446-0

Second, revised edition
Made in Europe, 2015

PHOTO CREDITS
© VG Bild-Kunst, Bonn 2015: Alexander Lichtveld, p. 18
© Henry Moore Foundation/The Bridgeman Art Library, p. 19

The Board of Education in Nichinan-city, Miyazaki p. 10 (below)
The Board of Education, Osaka p. 33
George Bouret, Courtesy of Lacoste Gallery fig. 56
Michele Brouet figs. 18, 19
The Cleveland Museum of Art fig. 57
Takeshi Fujimori p. 10 (above)
© President and Fellows of Harvard College p. 38
Andrew Lamoreaux fig. 11
The Museum of Oriental Ceramics, Osaka p. 17
Ikko Nagano figs. 1–6, 9, 10, 12–17, 20–52, 56, 58, p. 23
Geoff Spear figs. 7, 8, 53
Asako Takeda, PaLAM p. 22 (below)
TNM Image Archives p. 30 (below), p. 32
The University Museum, The University of Tokyo p. 30 (top)
Hiroki & Hideki Yamamoto p. 107

For general questions, please contact ARNOLDSCHE Art Publishers directly at art@arnoldsche.com, or visit our website at www.arnoldsche.com for further information.

Front cover: Slice of Earth, 2010 (fig. 56)
Back cover: KAZE, 2006 (fig. 28)

Contents

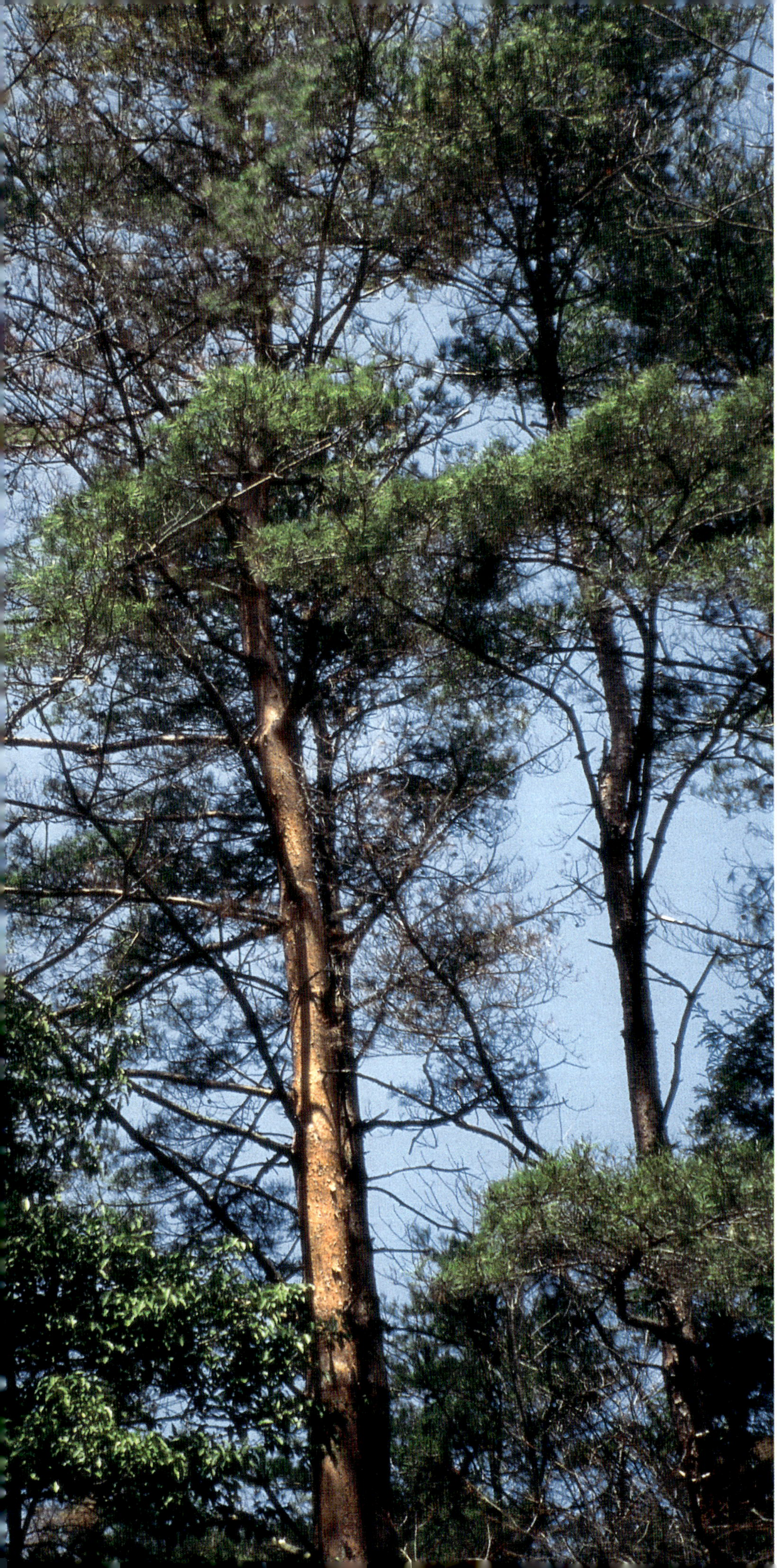

Tradition and Innovation in the Work of Yasuhisa Kohyama

SUSAN JEFFERIES

The bones of the old are legible (or visible or audible) under the contemporary skin. That's what produces the modernist dissonance.[1]

Yasuhisa Kohyama is a ceramic artist with a profound interest in the past. He has studied historical Japanese ceramics and admires the power of these pieces. He wants to capture this legacy, intuitively, and to draw upon their spirit in a way which is not alien to his own character and work.[2] Kohyama has taken two ancient traditions, wood-firing and hand-building and has devoted the last fifty-five years of his career to perfecting their use. Equally important is his embrace of contemporary life, and his bold and poetic use of line, mass, and form; he is fully aware of the sculptural possibilities available to him. A love of nature and a life-long interest in sculpture and architecture have also inspired his work.

Early Years

Yasuhisa Kohyama was born in 1936 in Shigaraki[3], one of the most important historical ceramic centres in Japan. During his school years, he enjoyed making realistic drawings of his friends and hoped to go to art school to be a painter, but his life changed at age ten with the death of his father in a bicycle accident.

Every time I fire, I've come to recognize that I am in Nature; I am a small part of Nature. Intently I watch Nature over and over again; working with clay, inspired by Nature, I am free to allow creation to happen, approaching the experience as the ancients did.

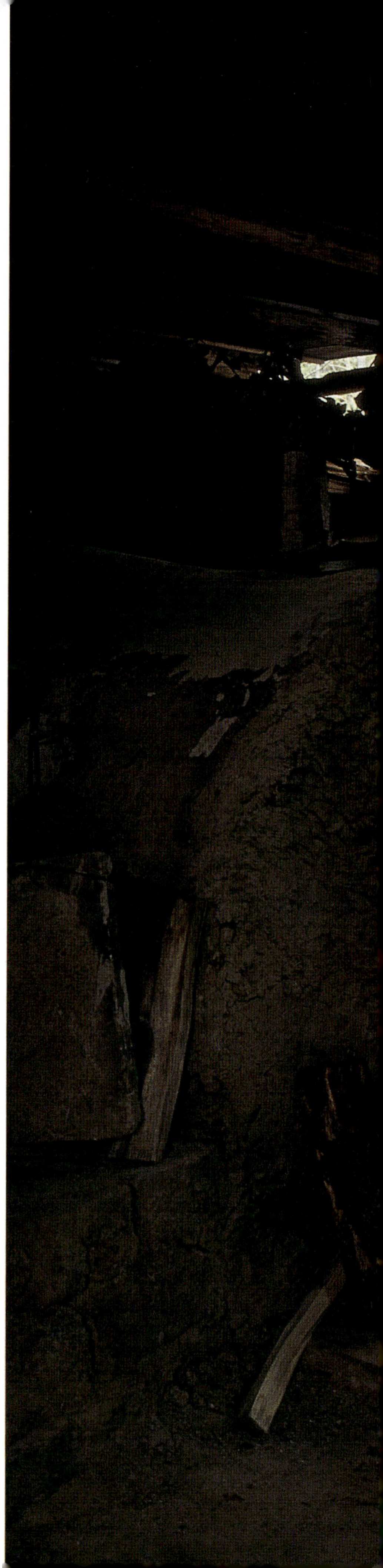

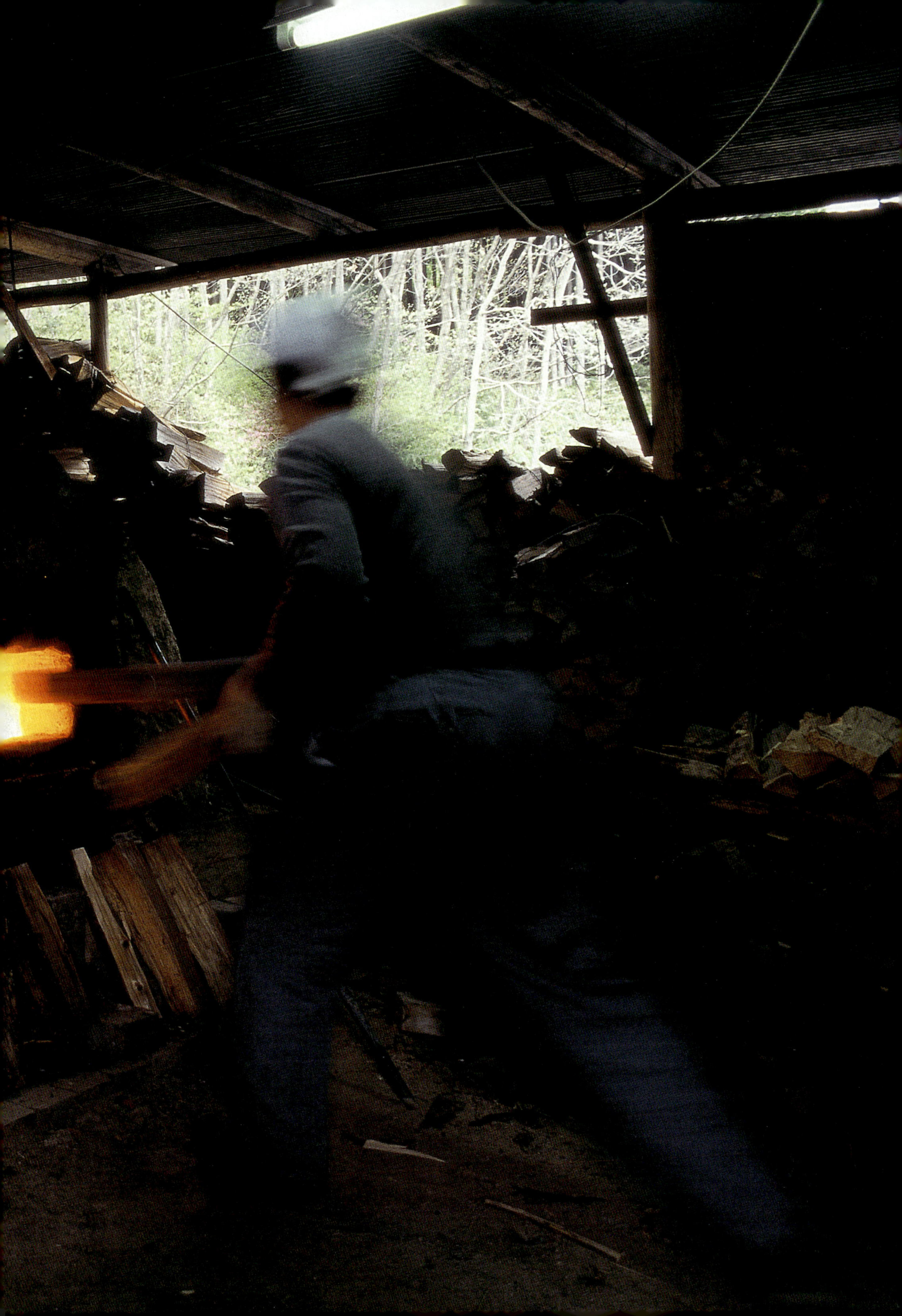

and then red pine, an oily wood that burns very hot. Between two hundred to three hundred bundles (36 x 36 x 40 cm long) of wood are needed to complete each firing.[30] Anagama kilns consist of a fire area at the front, where wood is fed into the kiln, then a stacking area[31] and a chimney at the back, which draws the fire and heat across the pots. Micro-climates are created in the chamber and the oxidizing and reducing atmospheres are in a constant state of flux, creating the exciting surfaces we associate with wood-firings. Over the years, trial and error become part of the potter's experience. A boldness of form is necessary to placate the fierceness of the fire. It is as if the character of the pot has to be worthy of its transformation and has to have the vigor to withstand the fire. All wood-firing potters feel a kinship with the concept of "a baptism of fire."[32] Artists seem to be happy to offer up their work to the fire, almost like a purification rite, and to have their own associations with the piece modified or at least tempered by the process. Extreme climatic conditions such as wind, rain, and snow can affect the results in the kiln and have been known to produce kiln disasters or unique, distinguished work. In 1972, a typhoon was blowing and played havoc with Kohyama's firing. The wind coming down the chimney and in through the kiln's orifices resulted in a lidded jar similar to those so highly regarded and used in the Japanese tea ceremonies in earlier centuries. This particular piece[33] with its traditional form and rough, primitive surface appears to be from another era, timeless, "born not made."[34] During the firing, controlling the oxygen intake can give a piece a primitive and uncontrolled quality, creating a sense of "life" on what might be a stolid form. When the piece is licked by the heat of the fire or a breath of wind, a subtle, elusive mark or memory is recorded on its surface. The placement of pieces in the hot or cooler parts of the kiln is of strategic importance. Because of the properties of the clay as well as the high heat, the atmosphere in the kiln, and the falling of the wood ash on the pots, warm colors as well as attractive markings can be captured on the surface of the clay. By stacking or placing pots against each other with wadding[35] in between to keep the pieces from sticking, attractive markings can be obtained (no. 9). Kohyama does not use a pyrometer or cones; he relies solely on a visual assessment of the color of the heat to judge the temperature and state of the firing.[36] He estimates a range of 1,280–1,350 degrees centigrade across the kiln with the wood ash melting at about 1,300 degrees. The blue-gray and red-orange colors develop in the mid-section of the kiln. In the back of the kiln, a heavily reduced atmosphere creates rich dark gray and brown colors.[37] It is often

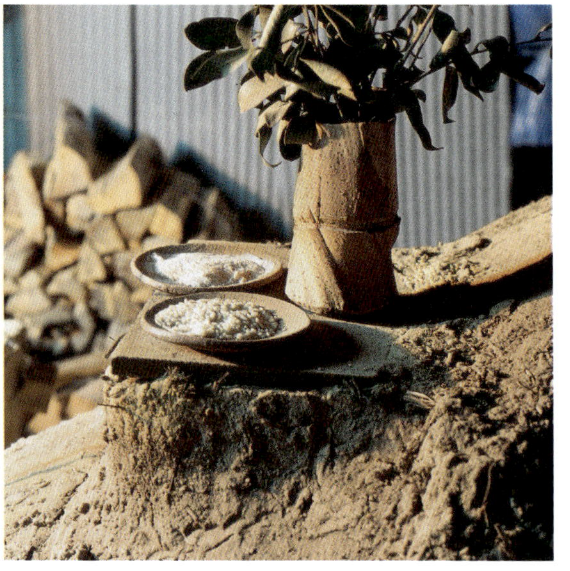

A kiln offering of salt, rice, and leaves of the Sakaki tree associated with the Shinto religion

necessary to fire pieces more than once to achieve the desired results. Kohyama always stacks the kiln himself with up to 100 pieces for each firing, depending on the size of the pieces. As is traditional, after finishing the stacking, he sprinkles sake and salt, prays, claps his hands twice, and bows—the firing then begins its week long cycle.[38] After reaching temperature, the kiln takes a week to cool down. The clay slurry is removed from around the door and the bricks are pried out. Each firing is an adventure and challenge, and it is thrilling when pieces are more exciting than expected. Although the process is exhausting, there is euphoria when a successful firing has been achieved. The unloading of the kiln can feed future ambitions and Kohyama for one is already thinking of what he'll do next.[39]

Travel, Friendships, and Exhibitions

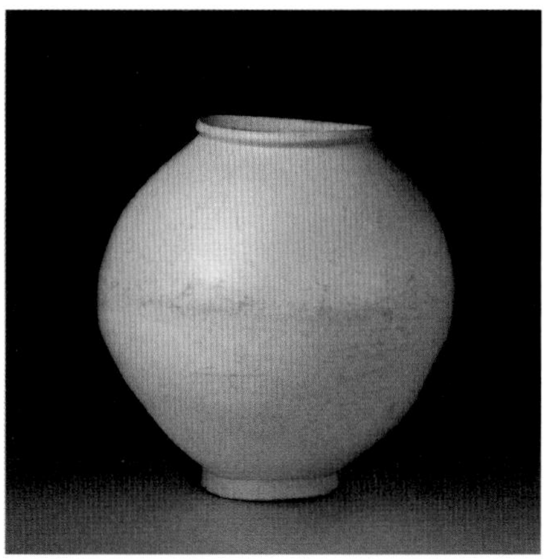

Korean moon jar, late 17th/early 18th century, The Museum of Oriental Ceramics, Osaka

Kohyama is an enthusiastic traveler and has worked in various locations worldwide as well as welcoming artists to his studio in Shigaraki. These travels and friendships have given him an opportunity to broaden his interests, to see new landscapes, and to meet other artists. In 1983 Kohyama travelled to Korea and saw the famous moon jars in the National Museum. These exquisite white vessels, made in the late 17th to 18th centuries of the Joseon dynasty (1392–1910), were named after the full moon and made from two bowls (one inverted), and joined at the centre. They are rare and much valued by potters for their form and delicate beauty. Over the course of his career Kohyama has returned briefly to this beautiful rounded shape, although his treatment of the neck and lip differ from its historical antecedents (nos. 9, 10, 11). In 1985, a Dutch ceramist, Alexander Lichtveld, came to work in Kohyama's studio for six months. This was an important period as it introduced Kohyama to European sensibilities and to Lichtveld's interest in geometric abstraction, as well as to a more experimental and sculptural approach to clay. Lichtveld in turn describes the experience with Kohyama as "changing his way of working and thinking."[40] *I found it inspiring how he worked in an intuitive direct way, the opposite of my way of working at that time. I used to plan my sculptures more in advance, more like an architect would do. I learned a lot about his way of working, and later it became also a part of my way of working. After all these years this experience is still a source of inspiration.*[41] Such was their regard that the two colleagues were able to arrange and help each other with exhibitions in their respective countries.

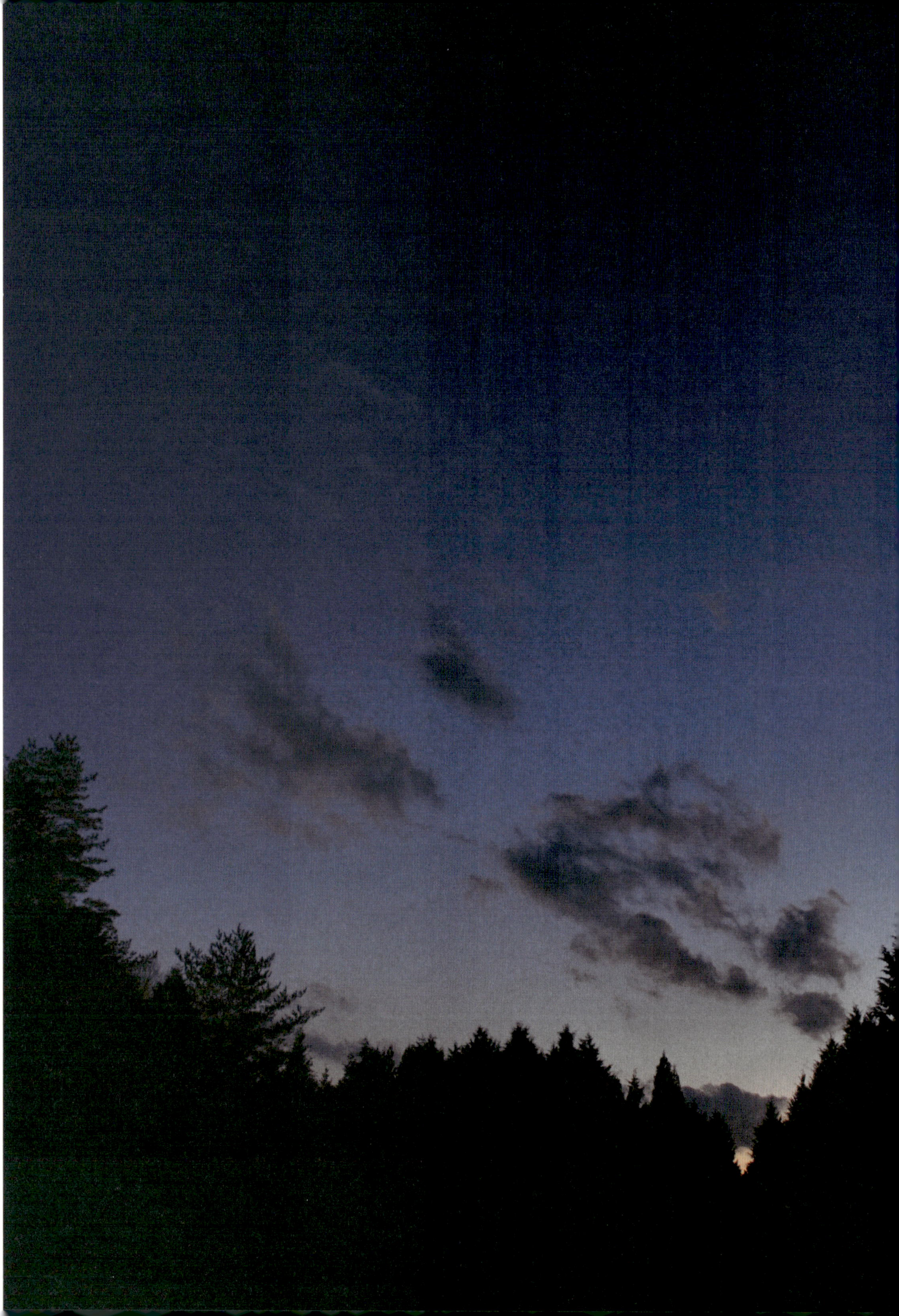

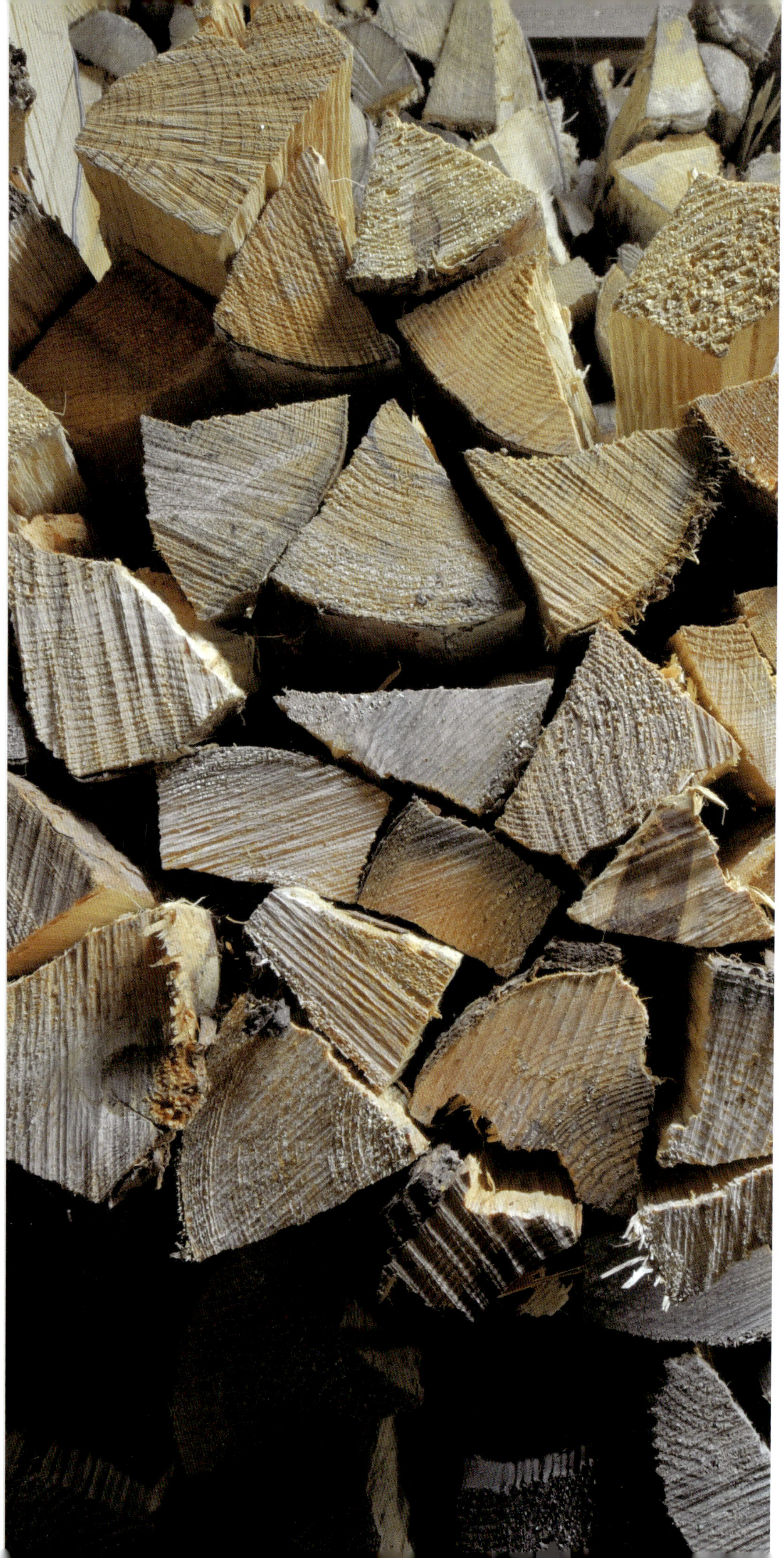

Kohyama-san and Japanese Ceramic History: Notes on "Suemono"

MICHAEL R. CUNNINGHAM

The observer of Kohyama Yasuhisa's oeuvre presented in this book will notice quickly its cohesive formal and textural vocabulary. Without referring to chronologies of production, it is apparent that an impressive range of ceramic shapes fills the landscape of his making. And their surfaces are remarkable. Japanese culture, despite its burnished modernity in Western eyes, has regularly eschewed such creative artistic range in favor of practiced traditional memory. Visual recognition courses deeply within the people there, as if a meditative glance toward individual, personal history were encapsulated therein. Be it materials or subject matter, "place" or familial lineage, visual language or cultural demeanor, the potters of the islands of Japan have for millennia been able to refer to these in their practice within vivid historical parameters. However, the particular challenge for modern potters has been the accommodation of Western aesthetic phenomena following the Meiji Restoration in the late 19th century, and the country's globally wrenching post-World War II exposure. The tensions between the classical and the new frame Kohyama-san's life and career, and highlight his ceramic responses to accepted norms of form-giving, as well as his determination to breathe into his hands clay visions released by encounters with an accessible "outside" world. Yet ambition in Japan, especially among commoners, has long been suspect and treated harshly, requiring for most an aesthetic program shouldering ever-shifting cadences of modernity with the recognizable classic, or the routine. No aspiring craftsperson has flourished in this country without acknowledging the "textbook" past in his or her work. Viewed as either a burden or learned freedom, such a reality results practically in a richly nuanced series of identity codes and associations, as well as interpretive systems that exist as accepted visual language on the archipelago, although persists as intriguing mysteries to most outsiders.

Kohyama-san has negotiated these interlocking landscapes of ceramic history, shifting cultural values and commercial industry with an eye both to economic viability and to an engagement with the new. His story, told elsewhere in this volume, is not exceptional in post-World War II Japan. But it is remarkable judging simply by a measured perusal of the clay objects before us—in our space or in our hands—that he has determined to form. They represent decisions arrived at amidst decades of engagement within Japan's clay culture—the most dynamic in the world—and an ambition to comprehend and embrace non-traditional ideas and imagery for inclusion in his life's work.

Just how one goes about actually accomplishing this endeavor is too daunting a task to convey here. But what follows represents an effort to provide the curious Western aficionado of clay with an introduction to the historical underpinnings of Japanese cultural identity. These comprise a few of the markers with which Kohyama-san has lived and interpreted for his own use, in life as well as in the marketplace of pots in Japan. Any practitioner of his generation has lived in vivid awareness of ceramic ancestry, but one which is particularly anxious in the modern era. Fresh currents of ideas and ambiguous values from beyond its shores as well as an unprecedented series of waves of archeological discoveries prompted by Japanese modernization efforts brought to light controversial objects and anthropological theories concerning accepted Japanese identity.

In this environment, Kohyama-san worked and deliberated largely on his own rather than as a member of an established ceramic family or ancestral village lineage. As such he was "swimming upstream," but also relatively free thereby to identify and select his course of creative actions and the web of aesthetic, as well as historic markers by which he preferred to guide his efforts. Of special significance is his deliberate choice of the term "suemono" to characterize his oeuvre. The ensuing notes are intended to help illuminate this obscure historical ceramic term and its important meaning in the cultural history of the Japanese archipelago and East Asia. Kohyama-san was not born into a family possessing a pedigree in ceramic culture. But he grew up in a well-recognized region of vibrant, historic ceramic history: Shigaraki, not far from Kyoto. His efforts to succeed in such an environment therefore embraced a search for authentic roots within that tradition for his own work.

Suemono: Some Background

In fact suemono is not a word recognizable to art historians in Japan or the West—unless they specialize in East-Asian archeology or ceramic studies (a rare species in the West). This is because suemono is a specialist's term found only in historical documents to describe the archipelago's first high-fired stoneware production, known popularly as "sueki" ware. Which is to say that modern (late 19th–20th century) nomenclature for this type of ware issued from archeological reports was subsequently adopted into academic vocabularies, followed by popular newspaper, book, and museum catalog publications, and has then been continuously employed as the modern term to describe such wares. But Kohyama-san's study of sueki ware, its antecedents as well as its literary evolution in the latter 19th and early 20th centuries included his scrutiny of both historical objects and written documents. He sought to understand the earliest language employed to identify the (suemono) ware as a means to learn the authentic historic record of suemono's origins and to fathom what characteristics of this ware established its identity for Japanese society at that time. In this way it would be possible to more clearly elucidate the historical and material identity of suemono and just how his work could be interpreted in relation to an important, discreet moment in ceramic history. This is the normal discovery process of historians as well as "creators," yet in this instance reveals the extent to which an individual Japanese potter will pursue his or her own search for contemporary authorship in the distant past of written language as well as artifact. Kohyama-san knew about Japanese stoneware history and sueki in particular because he lived in the vicinity of its modern archeological discovery, the region in western Japan known as the Kinai, roughly embracing the modern Osaka prefecture and its environs. Industrial and commercial expansion in the 1950s and 1960s prompted numerous archeological projects in the vicinity, which were routinely reported in the media. In turn these activities prompted exhibitions and publications, all of which enabled Kohyama-san to contemplate how to incorporate sueki ware's appearance and material features into his evolving oeuvre. What indeed are sueki ware's characteristics, and how does one begin to comprehend them in the context of the historical record? And more pointedly, what features did Kohyama-san identify for himself and his practice in clay as "suemono" in these recently unearthed objects?

Some History of Sueki Wares

The introduction of high-fired stoneware technology and its associated culture of artistic labor and civic usage represents a signal moment in Japanese cultural history and its relationship to the East-Asian peoples nearby. Following many thousands of years of a prosperous, widespread earthenwork defined by the Jomon (12,000 BCE–300 BCE) and Yayoi (300 BCE–300 CE) eras, the Kofun (300 CE–650 CE), or "burial mound" historical period, can be identified with Japan's modern state formation. This is the time of sueki ware's appearance on the archipelago. The archipelago's increasingly complex relationship with the more sophisticated peoples of the Korean peninsula as well as of mainland China continued. The transfer of people, new technologies, materials, and ideas had become for communities in Kyushu (to the west) and the Yamato region (present-day Osaka and Nara to the east) essential components in their respective social evolution toward organized agricultural units. Immigrants from the peninsula had settled in the archipelago by the later Jomon and upsurge for the Yayoi is clear, and travel no doubt occurred in the opposite direction too, as archeological finds along the southeast Korean coastline testify. Burial practices, similar grave goods, and exchange patterns in marine shells and prestigious metal objects between the Korean kingdoms of Paekche, Kaya, and the former Silla illuminate an active communication "highway" across a narrow sea passageway (of approximately 100 miles). By the 4th century the archipelago's immigrant population was not only significant, it represented a natural segment of tribal social structure, and had become enmeshed within the emerging elite families vying for regional political authority. Among the skilled workmen and artisans active in this setting were resident potters and kiln builders of the Yayoi era. Efficiently organized, they became instrumental in realizing the massive earthwork burial mounds (kofun) identified with the local elite. Kofun mound surfaces were arranged with constellations of large "haniwa" (cylindrical clay images), emblems of political and social status. Haniwa were produced by efficiently organized workers skilled in clay digging,

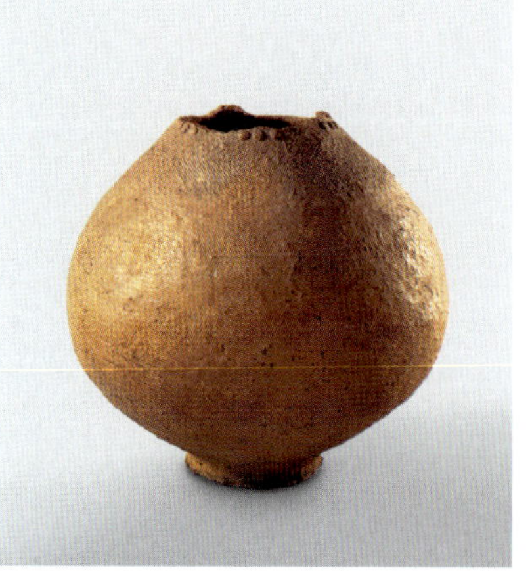

Jar, late Yayoi period, the University Museum, University of Tokyo

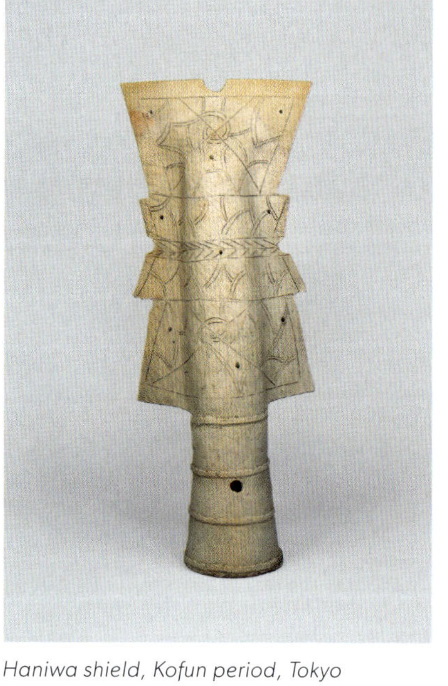

Haniwa shield, Kofun period, Tokyo National Museum

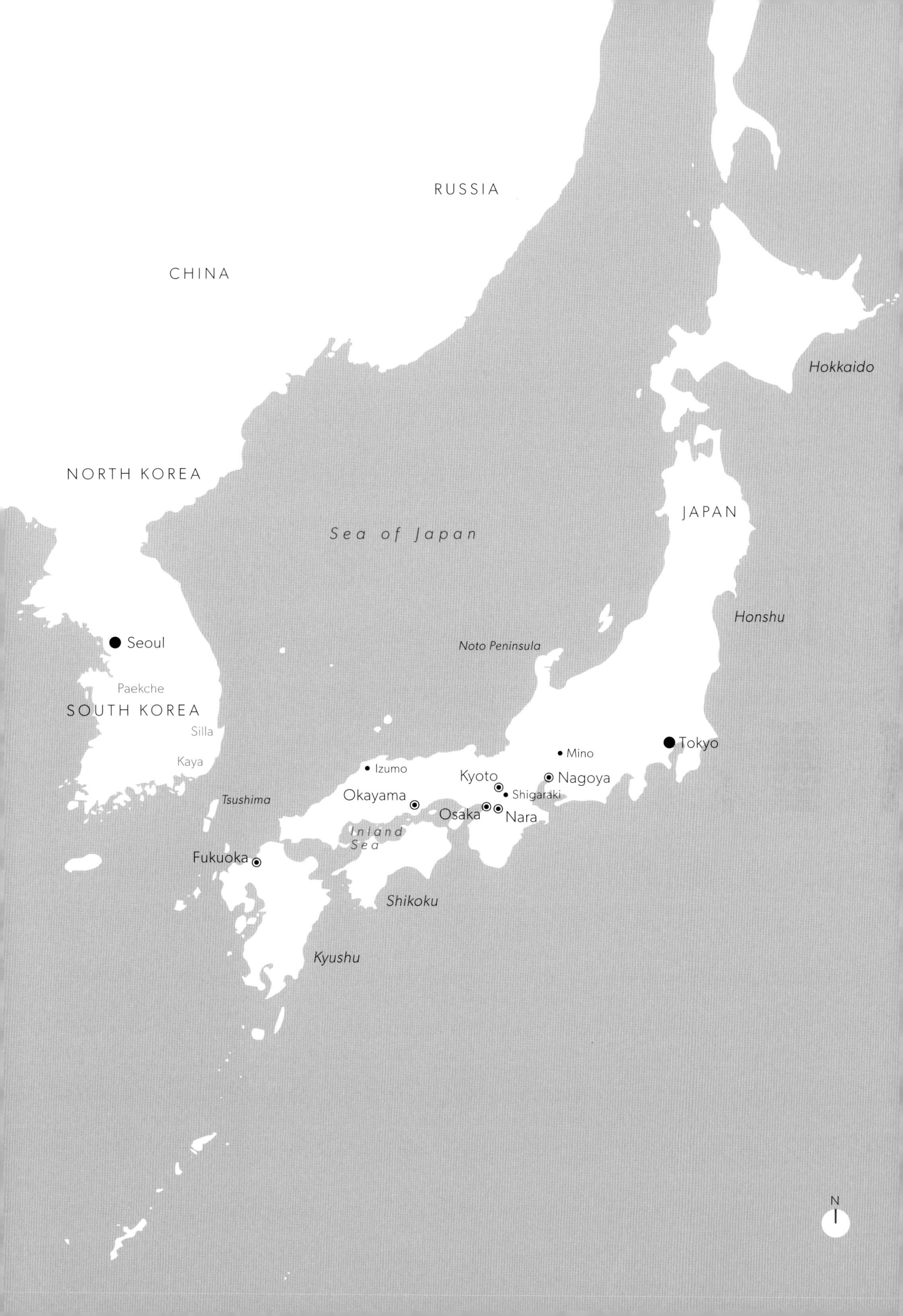
RUSSIA
CHINA
Hokkaido
NORTH KOREA
JAPAN
Sea of Japan
Honshu
Seoul
Noto Peninsula
Paekche
SOUTH KOREA
Silla
Tokyo
Mino
Kaya
Izumo
Kyoto
Nagoya
Shigaraki
Tsushima
Okayama
Osaka
Nara
Inland Sea
Fukuoka
Shikoku
Kyushu
N

clay refinement, and coiling techniques as well as wheel turning, surface decoration, and iconography. Associated village laborers supplied massive amounts of timber for fuel, and skilled technicians designed low-firing kilns capable of successfully producing many hundreds of earthenware haniwa, which were then transported to the summit of a kofun structure then rising in the vicinity. The proliferation of kofun building practices upcountry into the regions surrounding present-day Tokyo in tandem with a dramatic surge in their scale provides impressive physical evidence of the country's population migration and growth, as well as its concomitant social stratification. Embedded within these people were generations of immigrants from the peninsula, such as the haniwa-potter guild members or kiln masters, whose cumulative experience became essential to the success of regional elites as well as to the nascent indigenous ceramic trade spread across the archipelago. Thus the arrival from the peninsula in the 4th century of a new grayware ceramic body that was attractive in surface appearance and more durable than any ritual or utilitarian ware previously known represented a very special moment in material history on the archipelago. Native religious Shinto practitioners as well as political elites quickly grasped the symbolic potential of this new material and implications for form-giving. Sueki technology and personnel arrived both along sea and land routes. These dull, glistening graywares appear in the archeological record virtually simultaneously in Kyushu, Wakayama along the Inland Sea passageway, and in the Kinai-Yamato sphere. And not surprisingly, burial goods retrieved from elite kofun in these regions include both patently "Korean" graywares and "domestic" sueki ritual vessels, reflecting the rapid pace of transmission of this novel aesthetic genre, and its demanding technology, previously unknown on the archipelago. Closely resembling one another in shape typology, such alignments indicate the alacrity and the equanimity with which elite polities assessed them for prestige enhancement in secular and religious events within their communities. Rather quickly a professional guild of potters and—most significantly—kiln technicians ensconced on or newly arrived to the archipelago and found sufficient patronage to establish production sites across the islands. By the 6th century they were so embedded within society as to be indistinguishable from those skilled artisans around them, if we scrutinize the artifacts. Initial sueki production occurred in the hills around modern Osaka and quickly accelerated in the 5th and 6th centuries. Over six hundred kilns have been excavated in one area alone, measuring some twenty by nine kilometers in breadth. It is the result of modern excavation reports from here, Suemura

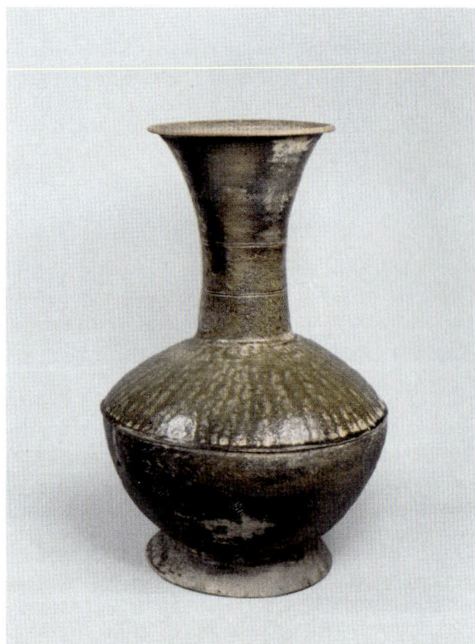

Sueki jar with tall neck, 7th century, Tokyo National Museum

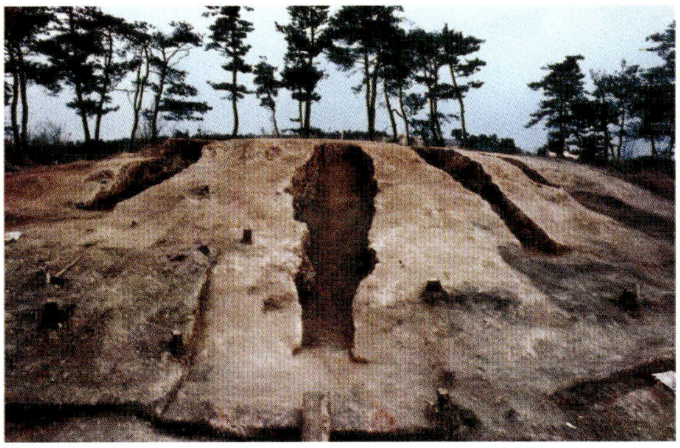

Suemura kiln excavation site

("Sue Village") and from the even more extensive Sanage excavations in the hills encircling the modern Nagoya area from which Kohyama-san derived his knowledge and his inspiration for the material fabric, surface appearance, weight, textures, and visuality of suemono as it came to public attention in the 1960s and 1970s. The reaction to these massive archeological findings reverberated with an excitement and curiosity that stirred people across many occupational pathways, not the least of whom were anthropologists, cultural historians, and, of course, potters. Suddenly an artifact appears in one's familiar material landscape, but with a different "look" and "feel" to it. Indeed these unearthed high-fired stonewares possessed novel surface palettes and architectonic structure. The bodies were durable and serviceable, unlike haniwa goods. And interpreters reckoned they derived in part from "other" clay traditions brought by ancestral elites as evidence of their sophisticated cultural and political interactions across the seas. Archeologists proposed that immigrant and then resident artisans had transmitted advanced technologies and experience to regional population centers. Sue production appears also to have evolved in a succession of temporal waves, in three distinct phases between the late 5th century and the early 11th century, although these shifts occurred at varying paces in distant geographical locations. Sanage's extensive presence upcountry dominated the ceramic industry for centuries, due largely to the character of its clay deposits and its access to land and sea distribution routes. Fuel was also abundant. Consumers favored the warm, hardened Sanage body and surface for their use. The wares from Suemura downcountry languished in contrast, due in part to their less attractive surface coatings of natural ash glaze. Utilitarian demand—principally food serving and storage—prompted the development of new shapes and vessel sets, beyond those known from the peninsula's repertoire. And the presence of a glossy green, ash-glazed surface came to replace the dry, matte-gray fabric of peninsular stoneware and its successors. The marketplace made a distinction between the two recognizable ceramic products based upon aesthetic preference, and in doing so ignited a ceramic legacy that endures to the present. And, not surprisingly, strong consumer demand spawned another important development by the 8th or 9th century: recipes for applying glazing mixtures directly onto vessel bodies, resulting in higher decorative success rates and shorter firing cycles. Meanwhile the single constant feature present over these several centuries of sueki production remained the all-important kiln. Whereas earlier Jomon and Yayoi-era firings took place in open-air ground settings or shallow pits covered

After one week of firing, just before I finish, I am fascinated by the flame, caused by the high temperature, which emanates from the kiln's chimney. That color is red with a little purple—like the cardinal peony—and clear. I wish for the birth of new life. What did the ancient potter think on seeing this flame?

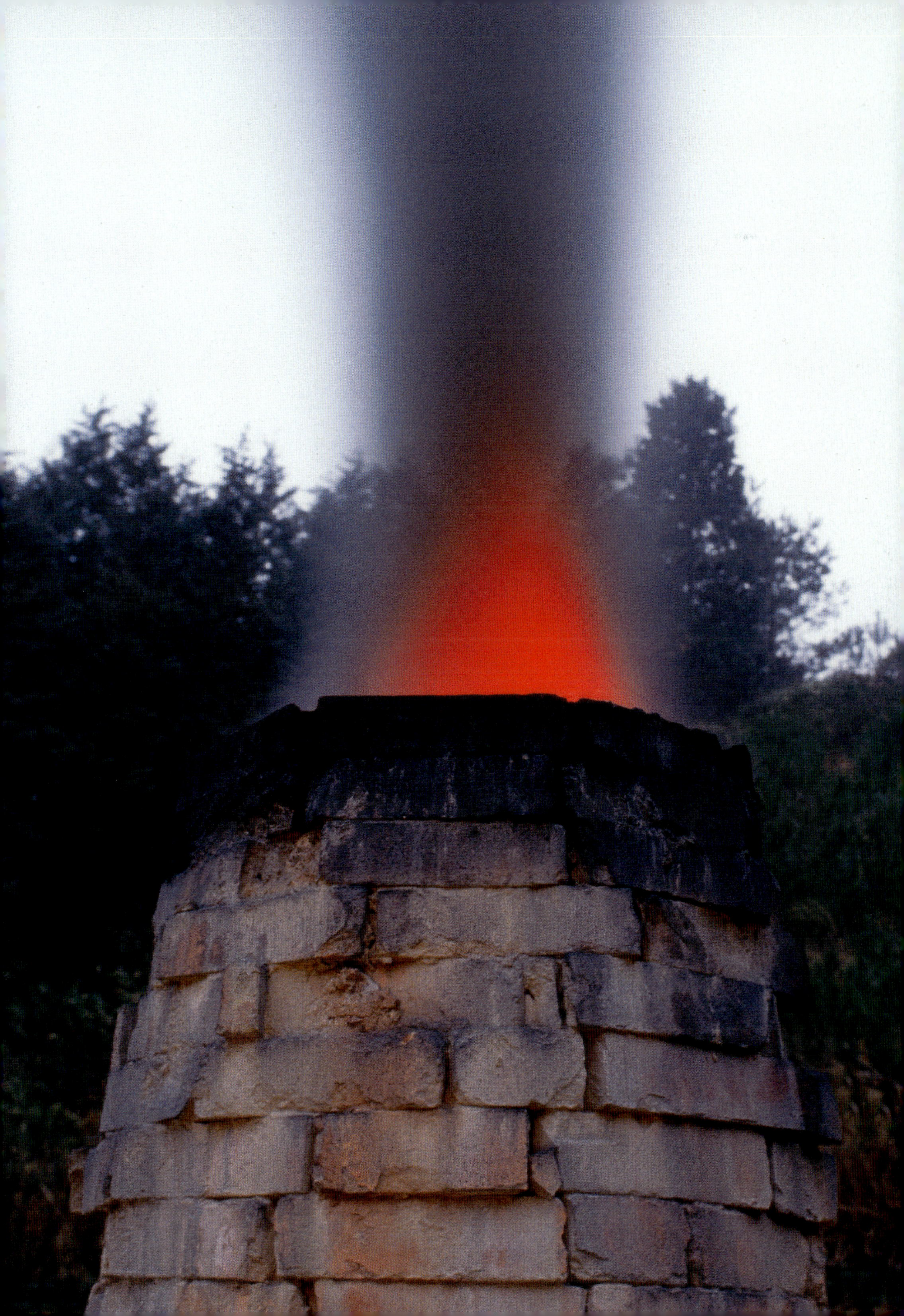

SINGLE CHAMBER, SLOPING TUNNEL KILN (HISTORIC ANAGAMA)

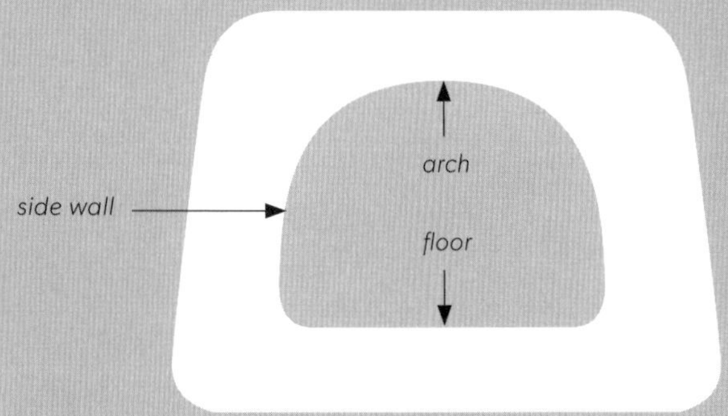

(cross section A–A′)

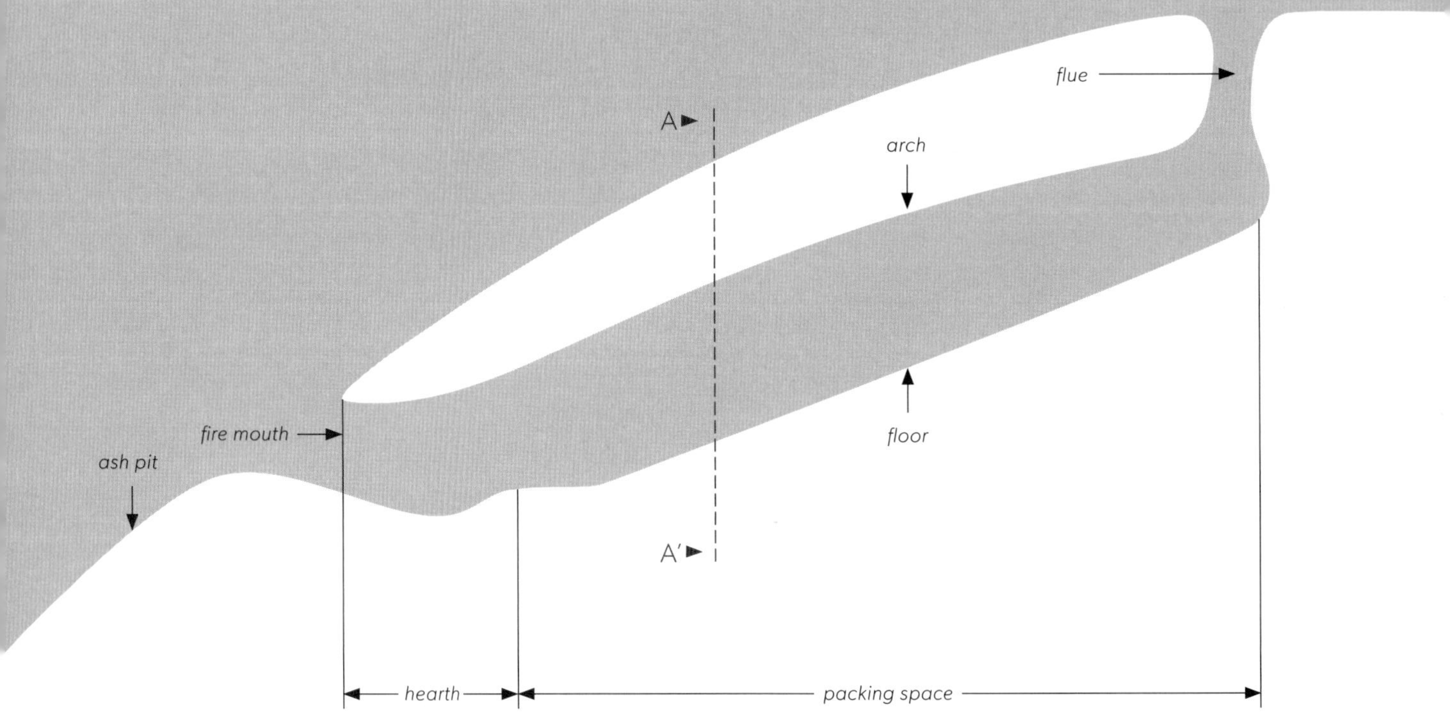

with combustibles, immigrant kiln builders shared their knowledge of excavating trenches, subsequently roofed, along hillsides so as to induce a natural updraft in the elongated chamber. Wares were stacked on the earthen floor. Then, simple tunnels were excavated in these slopes with a hole at the terminus of the tunnel space to serve as a venting chimney. Wood was pushed into the mouth and ignited, filling the single chamber with rising heat waves amidst a sooty atmosphere of organic combustibles. The next, crucial episode in kiln design arrived via the peninsula, and formulated a single chamber with stepped interior floors rising dramatically in tandem with the rising slope upon which the free-standing kiln chamber was constructed. This is the classical "anagama kiln" (tunnel kiln), and its essential design features traveled rapidly throughout the archipelago along with the immigrant peninsular technicians who were familiar with the details of its construction and its successful use, starting in the 5th century. By the 7th century anagama design had spread throughout the archipelago and had evolved to include double-mouthed openings and increases in chamber capacities. These design improvements did not alter the basic anagama accomplishment: the creation of an atmosphere in which temperatures of about 1,100 degrees centigrade could be achieved and then sustained using wood fuel. In such a fierce environment, clay bodies vitrify, producing hardened bodies, whose walls become non-porous, an enormously significant feature in agriculture-dependent societies. It is thought that the initial anagama "know-how" arrived in the 5th century via immigrant technology from the Kaya kingdom in southernmost Korea. Here, too, knowledge of iron ore and casting techniques flourished, in contrast to the archipelago where sources for this material were unknown at that time. Cast-iron ingots became precious trade items during the later Yayoi and then Kofun eras, and immigrants experienced in iron-casting techniques arrived during the Kofun to jump-start this technology for an increasingly agriculture-dependent society needful of more efficient tools. Anagama design and usage sits comfortably in this historic landscape of materials transfer. Domestic Sue kiln workers and potters in turn were able to achieve sustained, economically successful production rates for several centuries (6th–12th) and, along the way, manage to provide an aesthetic norm of appearance for their clientele who could discern amongst comparable utilitarian products. The archeological record tells us that sueki wares traveled about, from Kyushu to Izumo to Wakayama to Nara to the Noto Peninsula to Mino, to the highlands of Nagano and well beyond into the northern provinces. Sanage wares prevailed in taste apparently, and its many hundreds of workshops are responsible for the dark-bodied, thin, green-glazed surfaces which established a Kofun- and then early Heian-era aesthetic goal for producers and consumers alike. But there existed in actuality a variety of "looks" within the sueki vocabulary, apart from the vocabulary of shapes available. These surface tonalities ranged from brownish gray to dark —almost black—glistening surfaces bearing melting rivulets of green ash glaze translucencies—and many more variations in between, all due to the normal vagaries of any anagama firing. What linked them together as sueki or suemono, a more generous term for the typology, was their stoneware fabric, altogether distinct from the previous Yayoi genre. Kohyama-san settled upon a dry, unassuming sueki skin for most of his oeuvre, one virtually devoid of the thick, green wood-ash rivulets that have been so intimately associated with the historical sueki, and then later with the medieval "six kilns" aesthetic in Japanese ceramics. His clay bodies however exhibit a range of surface tonalities, and purposely so, but the thin glazing effects of their surfaces remain within rather strict parameters. This is a reference to historic peninsular traditions, either from Kaya (dark-bodied palette) or Silla (lighter, grayish-toned bodies virtually devoid of visible glaze) and their later descendants on the archipelago in later Kofun times. While the success of sueki production over the centuries became evident in modern time, it also revealed the rich complexities of the ware's visual appearance, far beyond what had been known or accepted by historians before then. Thus, richly glazed pieces that had already entered the canon of sueki ware and were prized by collectors and tea practitioners were joined by a whole range of plainer- looking "cousins." The understated, peninsular-based type in light gray or even brown tonalities surfaced to challenge established views of fundamental sueki features. Also in flux came basic issues of Japanese aesthetic identity in relation to those derived from East-Asian precedents, as well as many more topics, from anthropological to technological, and beyond. Interestingly, the sueki genre largely disappeared from public view among ceramic devotees due to the abiding aesthetic preference for richly glazed, sturdily formed vessels associated with the six historic medieval kilns. Abetted by the influential tea taste culture and the various bonsai (flower arrangement) school recommendations, modern potters paid scant attention to sueki ware's potential for their own creative purposes. They were also focused on Western sculptural developments of the 1960s. As a consequence, sueki's discovery languished here and there in archeological journals and museum gallery vitrines. Luckily for Kohyama-san, the historic unearthings in the Kinai-Yamato regions did surface in local

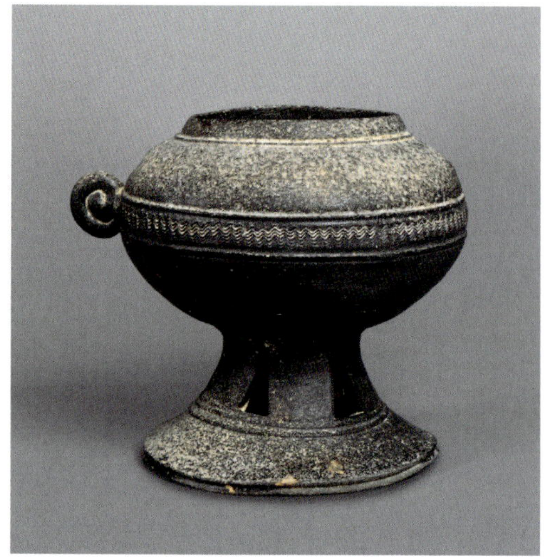

Pedestal Vessel Flaring Base, Whorl Handle, and Abstract and Openwork Decoration, 5th–6th cent. Harvard Art Museums/Arthur M. Sackler Museum, Partial gift of Maria C. Henderson and partial purchase through the Ernest B. and Helen Pratt Dane Fund for the Acquisition of Oriental Art, 1991.500

archeological, university, provincial, and national institutions for him to consider in his own work, and at a pace conducive to his study and absorption. Considered in this terse way, Kohyama-san's appreciation of the suemono cultural tradition bears notice. Clearly he has surveyed the archeological records of Jomon, Yayoi, and then Sueki as they have become exposed and subsequently interpreted during the last fifty years. He has also examined this continuum in relation to later Japanese ceramic traditions, which by and large emphasize explicitly decorated surfaces for their visual impact. In contrast to such approaches Kohyama-san has employed sueki's understated, barely glazed, rather dry surface aesthetic to advance his own work. Bodies exhibit subtle, richly varied tonal hues without dramatic gestures. Clearly his mastery of assorted clay mixes and his experience stacking and supervising the firing of his anagama appears in the oeuvre for all to consider. It is especially gratifying to see and to hold, as it conveys not only a personal history of clay but also a finely tuned, secure grasp of ceramic history on the archipelago, one not commonly acknowledged there.

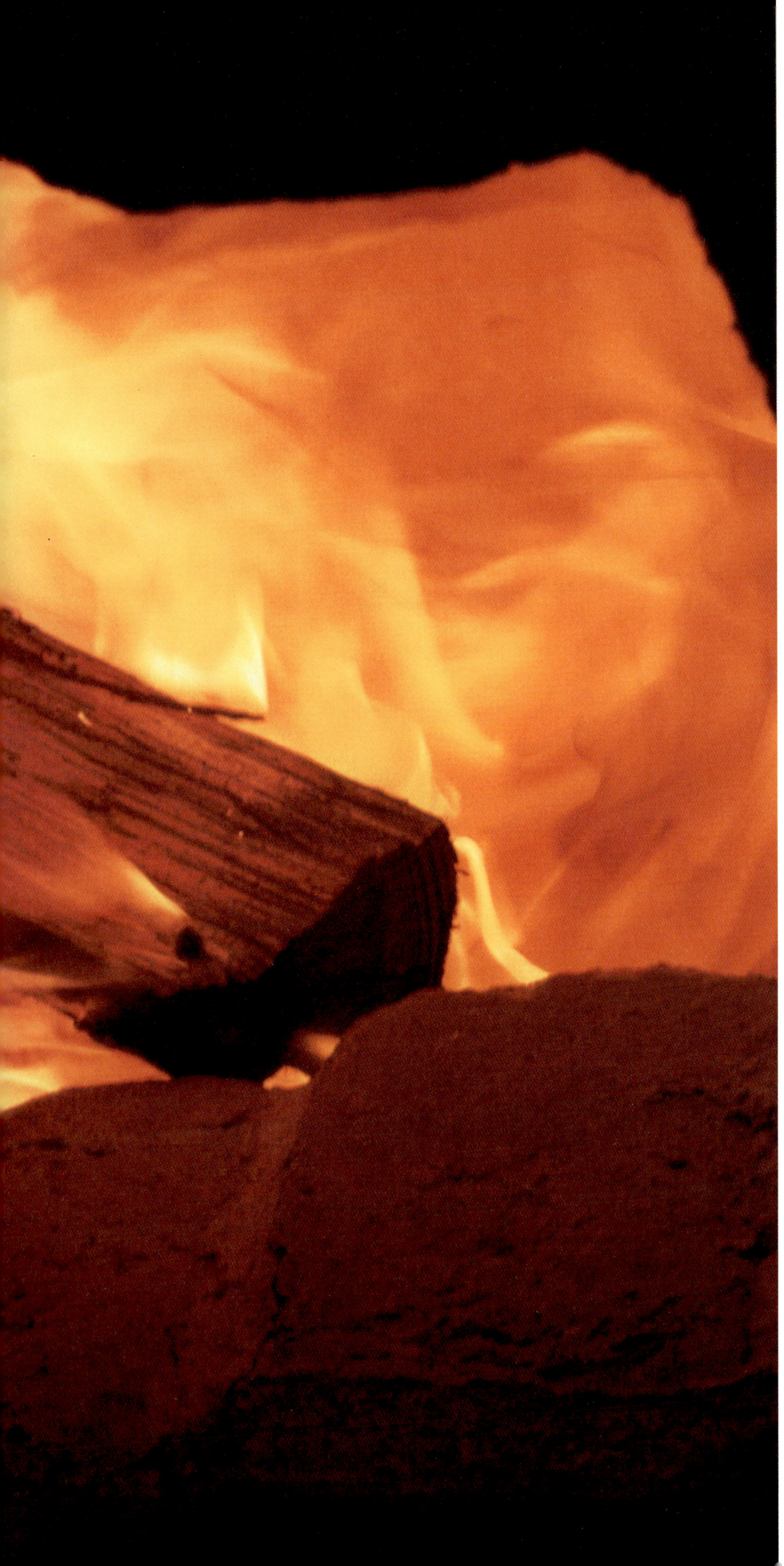

Yasuhisa Kohyama: The Art of Ceramics

YOSHIAKI INUI

Japanese ceramics have been subject to Chinese and Korean influences for many centuries. From the second half of the 16th century—the Momoyama period—Japanese ceramics have evolved from those influences, creating a style unique to Japan. One of the most important characteristics of Japanese ceramics is the very clay itself. Its peculiarity can be particularly appreciated when it is left unglazed. Another characteristic is the asymmetrical shapes. In contrast, for example, Chinese potters of the Song era made everything very symmetrical, whereas tea bowls, flower vases, and suchlike from the Momoyama period were violently distorted or boldly cut. This original Japanese style is not found anywhere else, not in Europe, China, or Korea. Yasuhisa Kohyama's work possesses an abundance of this original aesthetic quality. His work is made exclusively of Shigaraki clay, which is a little rough as it contains small stones and is unglazed. Its sandy surface invites people to touch it. We can best appreciate the originality of Kohyama's work by both handling and looking at it.

Because his work is never fragile, the rough clay adds to the totality of his creations. All his work is fired at a very high temperature, 1,250 degrees centigrade, and they come out physically hard and looking like stone. In some cases they emerge a beautiful brown color tinged with red, which gives them a very warm quality. By using these materials, Kohyama's work gives the impression of complexity. The combination of intensity, strength, and warmth gives expression to new works. In general, the form of his work is comparatively concise.

All the works in this publication show simplicity as well as originality. Many geometric forms are used, but they are nevertheless asymmetrical and delicately different. The rich variation of Kohyama's work is a most noteworthy feature of his creative abilities. His intense energy flows through his hands and into the clay, creating original works of art. During the cutting of the surface of an object there is a moment of intense energy that is transferred to the object of creation. People viewing his work feel the impact of the power and freshness of it. Time, speed, and movement are condensed for a moment and stamped into the clay. The essence of Kohyama's work is a combination of physical aesthetics and the transfer of his energy, which gives each piece a unique life of its own.

His work, in the orthodox tradition of Japanese ceramics, conforms to the character of the clay and free creation. Because this dynamic creation was born from the intense connection between the clay and the artist, we can call it innovative, yet innovation is just part of what makes his work fresh. In short, Kohyama's work is strictly modern but based on tradition. Kohyama's works are mostly functional pieces, bottles, flower vases, and plates. Nevertheless, their strong independent shape and dignity means they can also be appreciated as artworks. Japanese contemporary ceramics treads a narrow path between the pressure of centuries of traditional style and the modern styles of today. It is fighting hard to find a way out of this conflict, but Kohyama always achieves excellence.

Reprint of an article by the author published in *Kohyama and Tanaka: Contemporary Ceramics and Textile Art from Japan*, Leeuwarden: Museum het Princessehof, 1992.

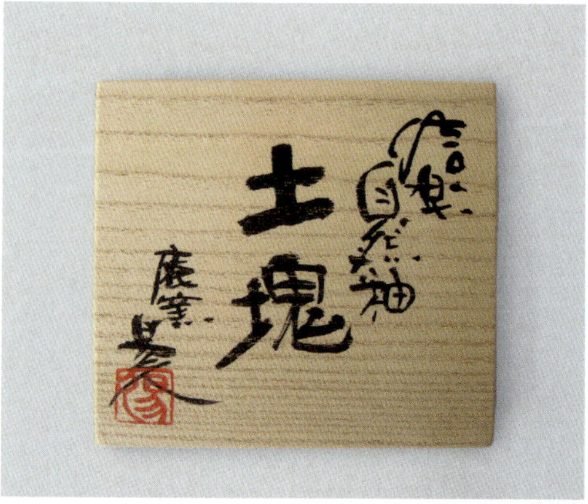

Box with calligraphy by Yasuhisa Kohyama

Japanese / English:

Shigaraki Shizenyu / natural glaze

MENTORI / Cutting
BACHI / Plectrum
SORA / Space
TSUBASA / Wing
TSUCHIKURE / Lump of Clay
KAZE / Wind
DANPEN / Fragment
HOMURA / Flame
DOKI NO NAKAMA / Fellows in Earthenware
SUEMONO / Ancient Ceramics

1 Shigaraki Shizenyu, Large Jar, 1982 ······· 25 × 25 × 35 cm (9.8 × 9.8 × 13.8 inches) ······· The Shigaraki Ceramic Cultural Park, Shiga

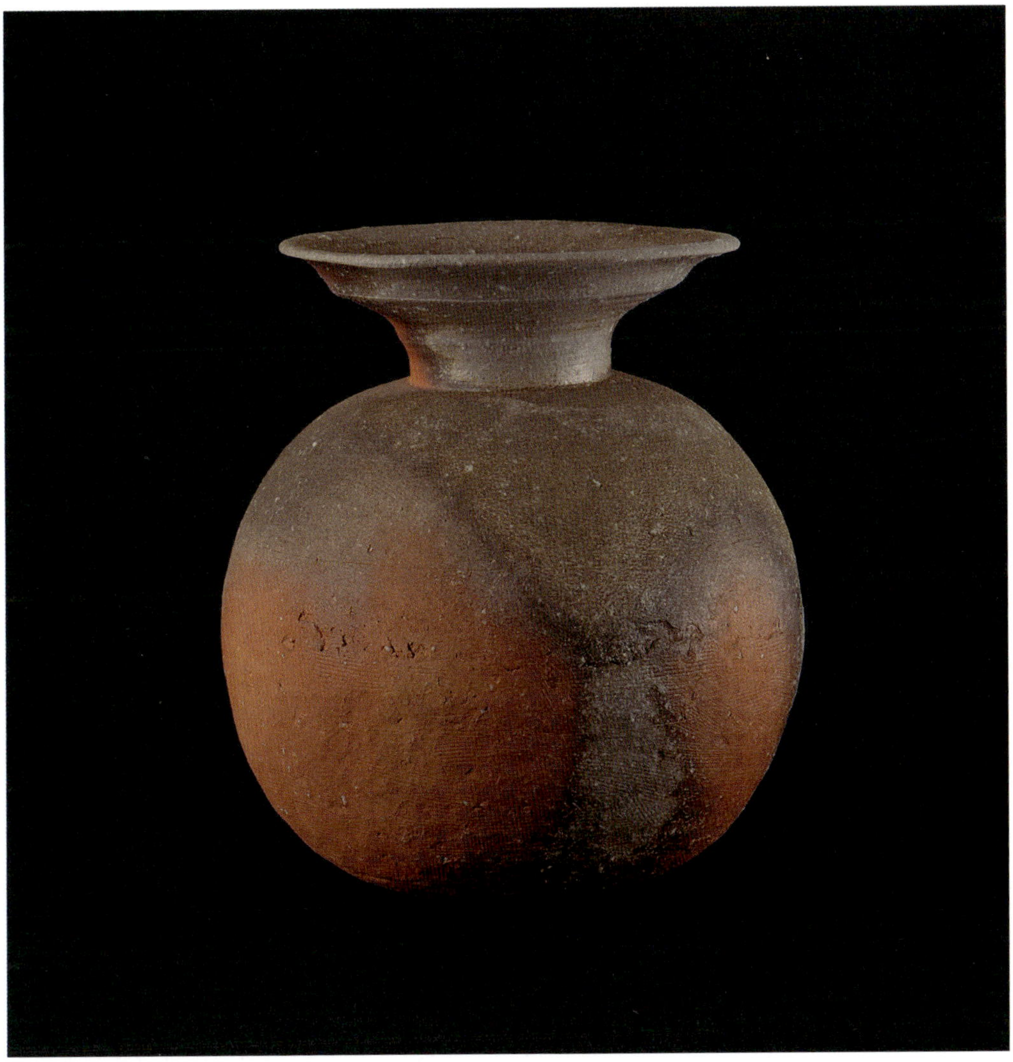

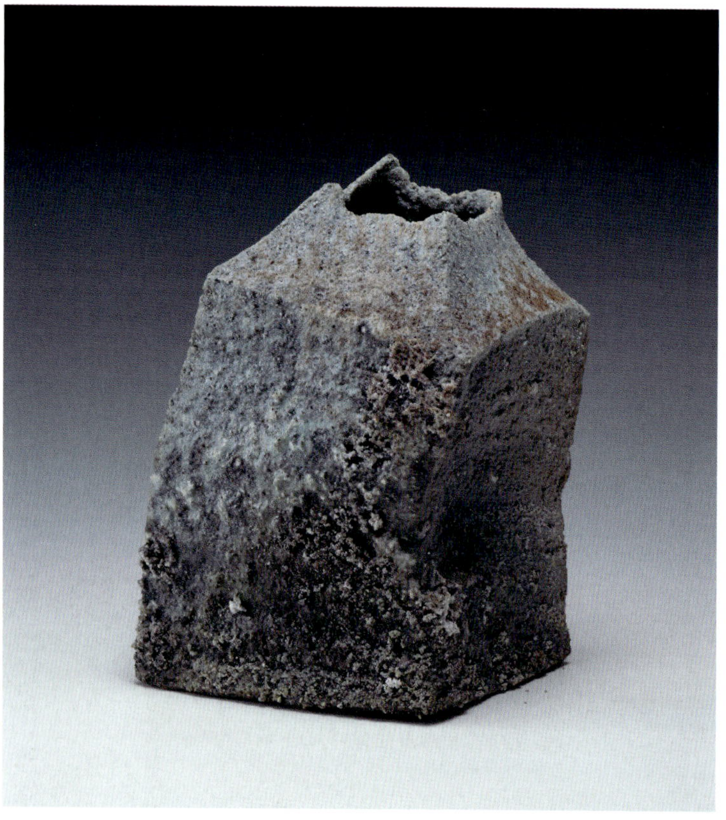

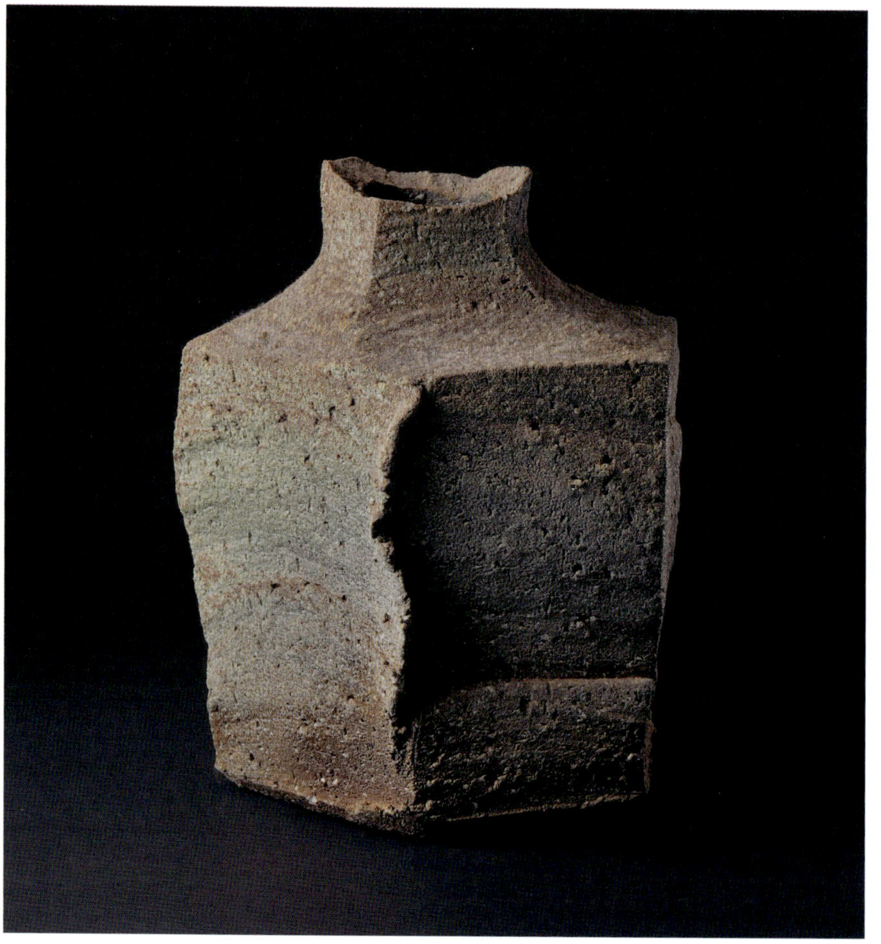

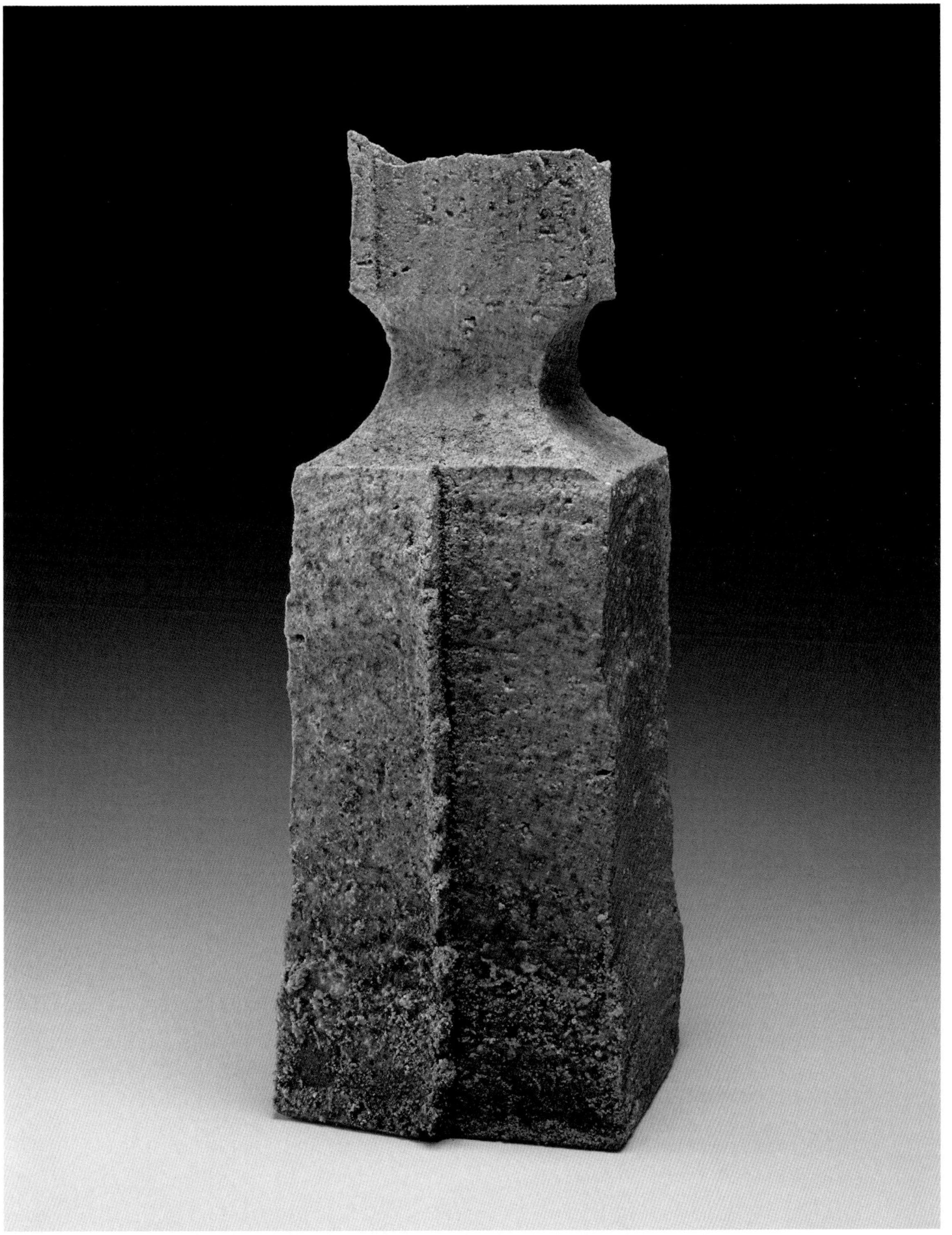

2 Shigaraki Shizenyu MENTORI Flower Vase, 1994 ······· 15.5 × 14.5 × 21.4 cm (6.1 × 5.7 × 8.4 inches) ······· Private Collection

3 Shigaraki Shizenyu MENTORI Flower Vase, 1987 ······· 23 × 15 × 30 cm (9.0 × 5.9 × 11.8 inches) ······· Private Collection

4 Shigaraki Shizenyu MENTORI Flower Vase, 1994 ······· 17.8 × 17.8 × 45.7 cm (7 × 7 × 18 inches) ······· Brooklyn Museum, New York

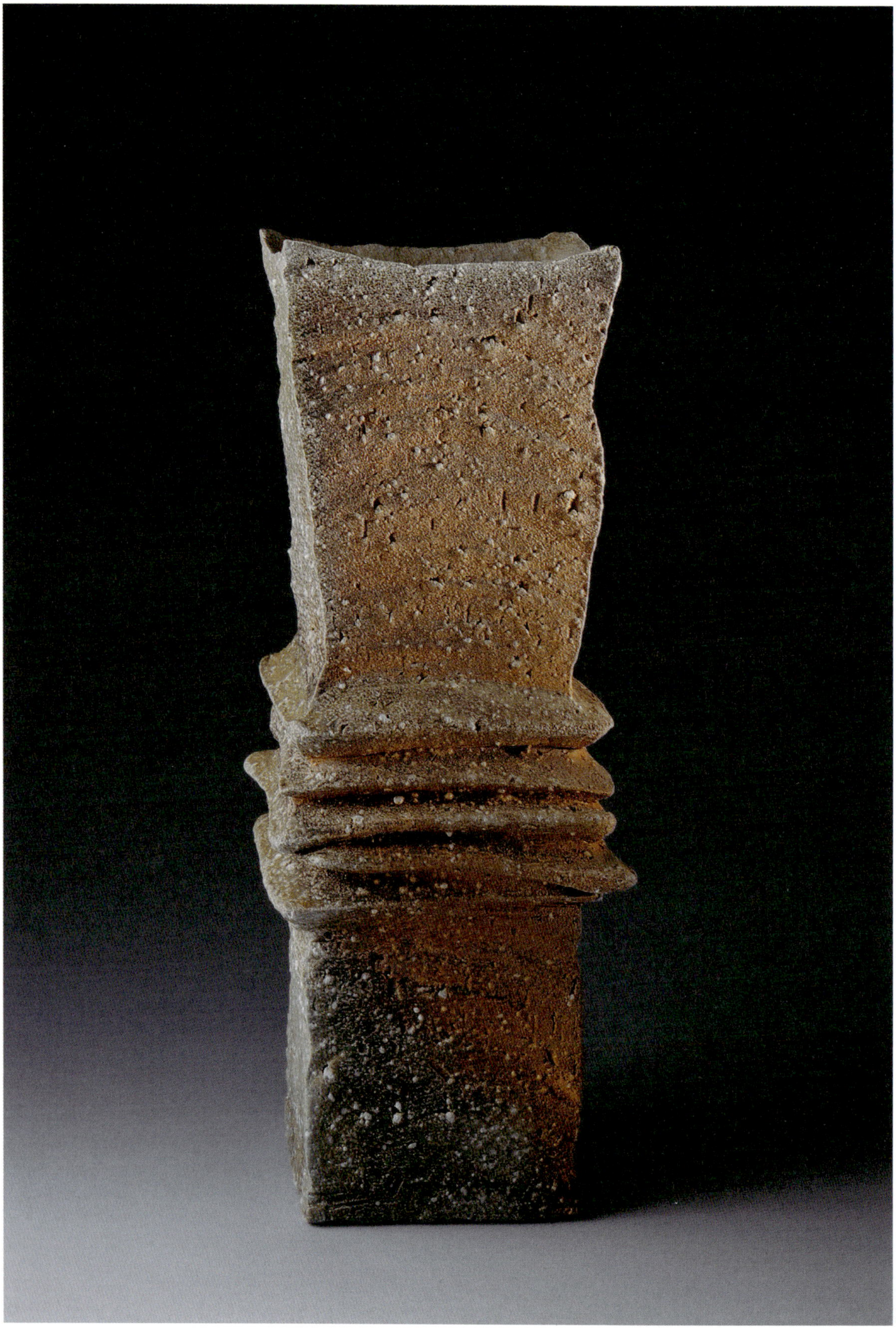

5 BACHI, 2010 ······· 20 × 16 × 51 cm (7.9 × 6.3 × 20.0 inches) ······· Private Collection

6 Shigaraki Shizenyu MENTORI Flower Vase, 1973 ······· 14 × 14 × 28.5 cm (5.5 × 5.5 × 11.2 inches) ······· Private Collection

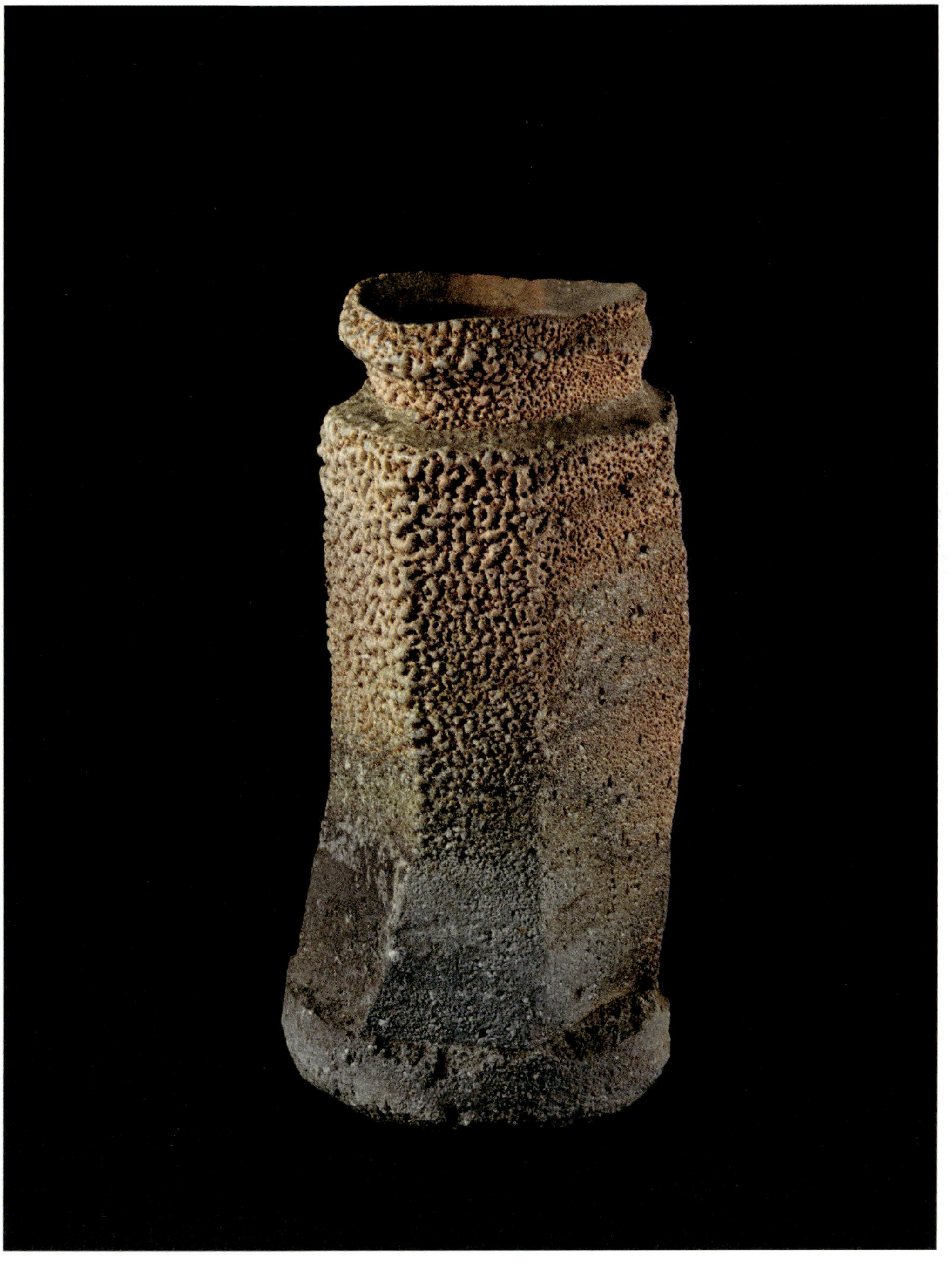

7 Untitled, 1998 (front and back view) ······· 9.7 × 9.7 × 29.2 cm (3.8 × 3.8 × 11.5 inches) ······· Samuel and Gabrielle Lurie Collection, New York

8 Untitled, 1995 ······· 17.3 × 17.3 × 59.5 cm (6.8 × 6.8 × 23.4 inches) ······· Samuel and Gabrielle Lurie Collection, New York

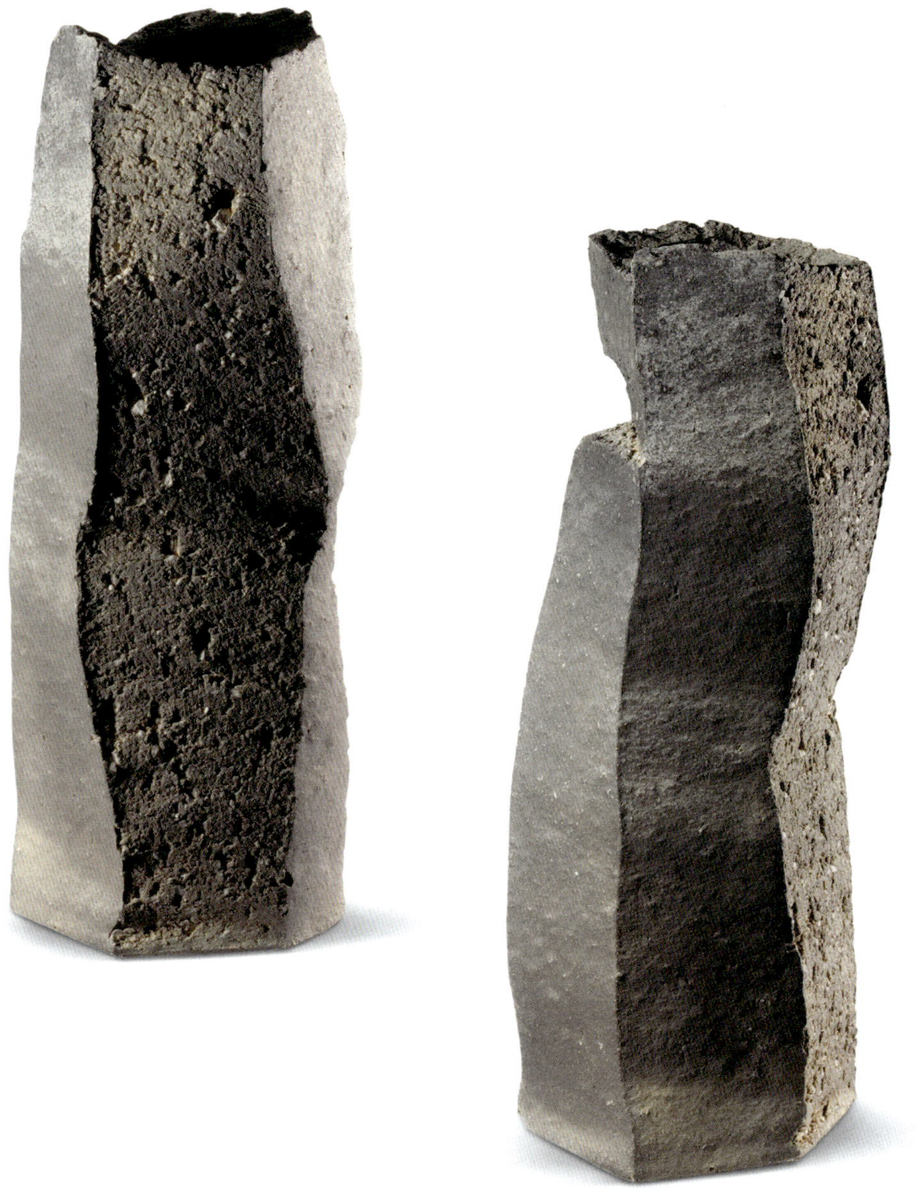

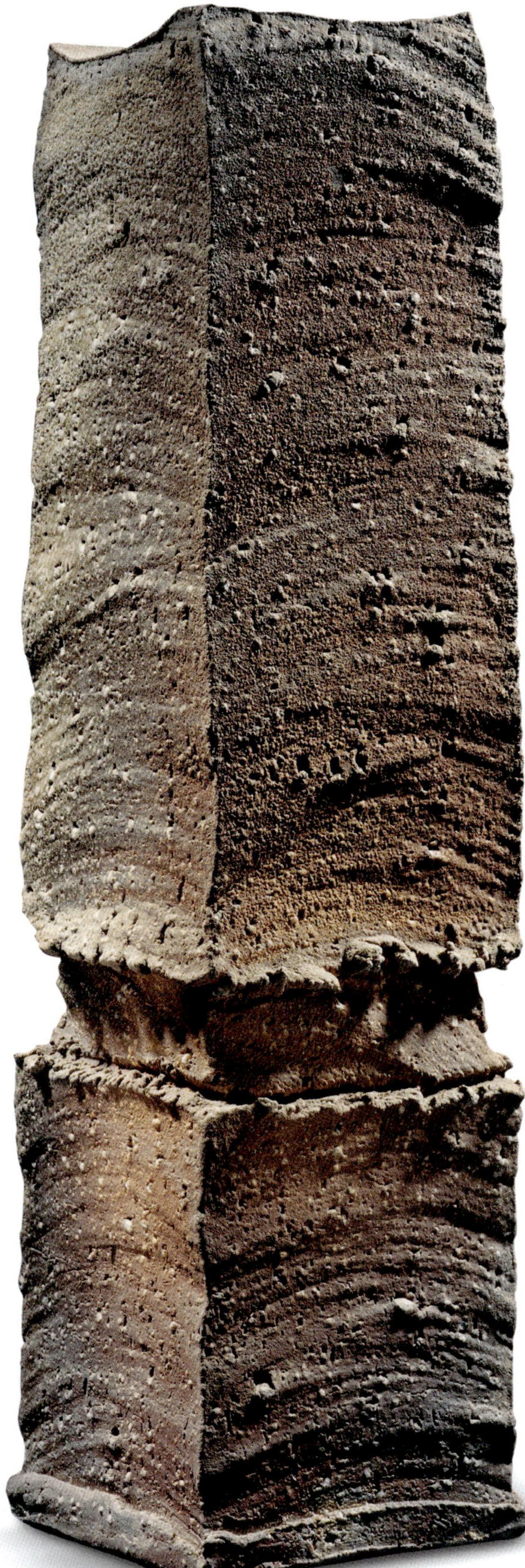

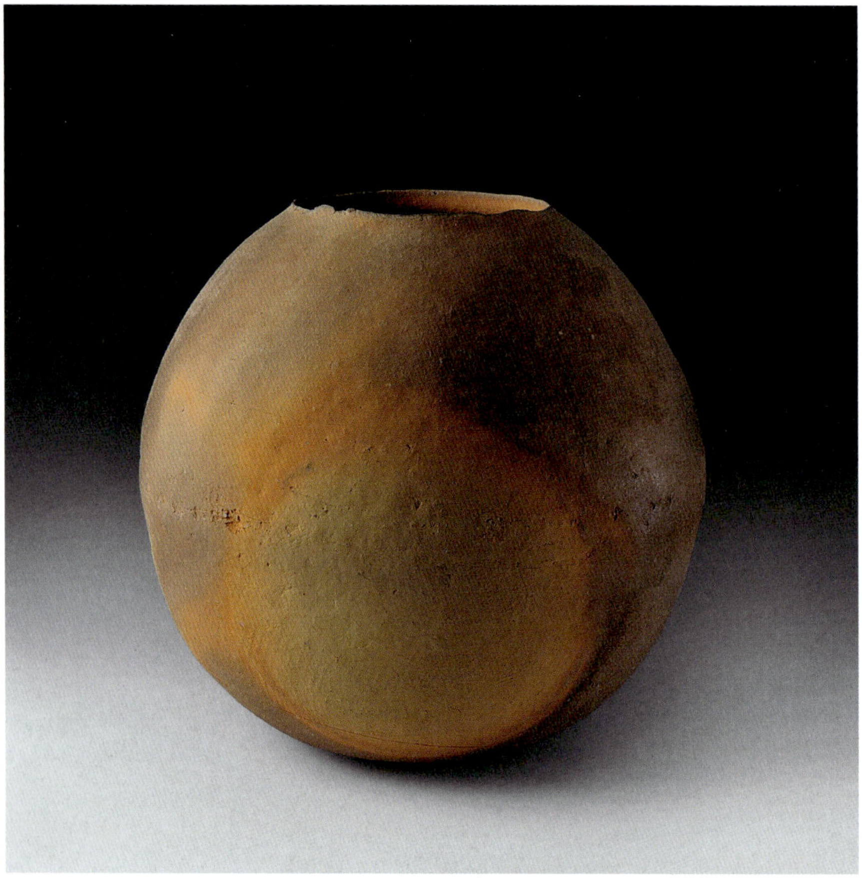

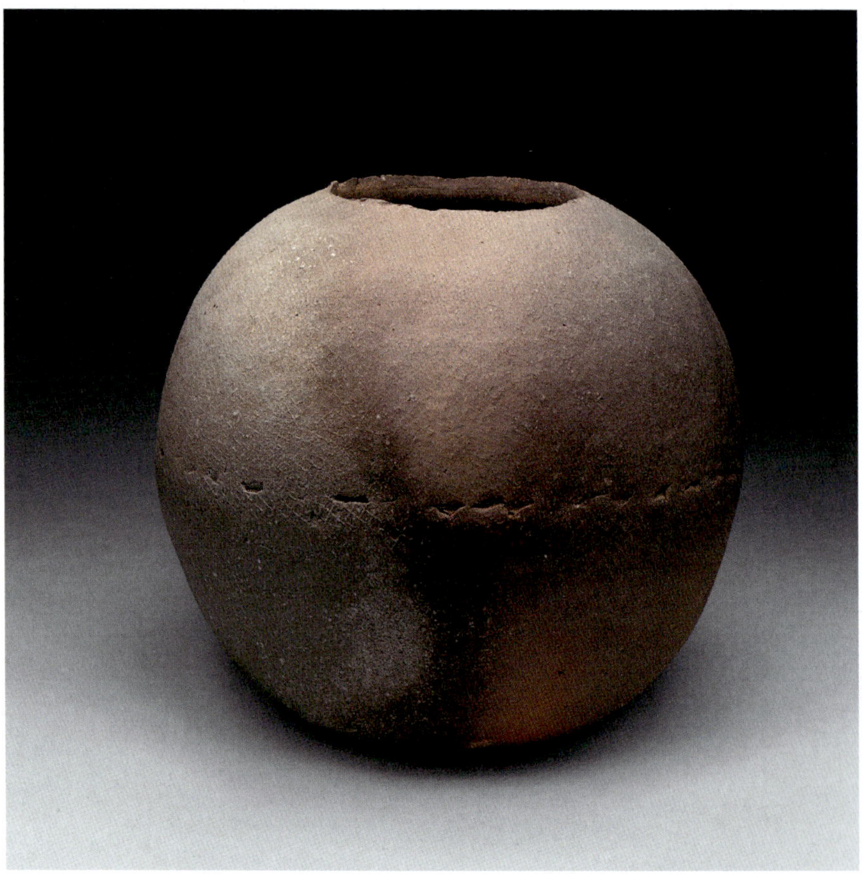

9 SORA, 2011 ······· 45 × 45 × 45 cm (17.7 × 17.7 × 17.7 inches) ······· Collection of the artist

10 Shigaraki Shizenyu, Large Jar, 1992 ······· 42 × 42 × 45 cm (16.5 × 16.5 × 17.7 inches) ······· Private Collection

11 SORA, 2009 ······· 51 × 51 × 51 cm (20 × 20 × 20 inches) ······· The Los Angeles County Museum of Art, Los Angeles

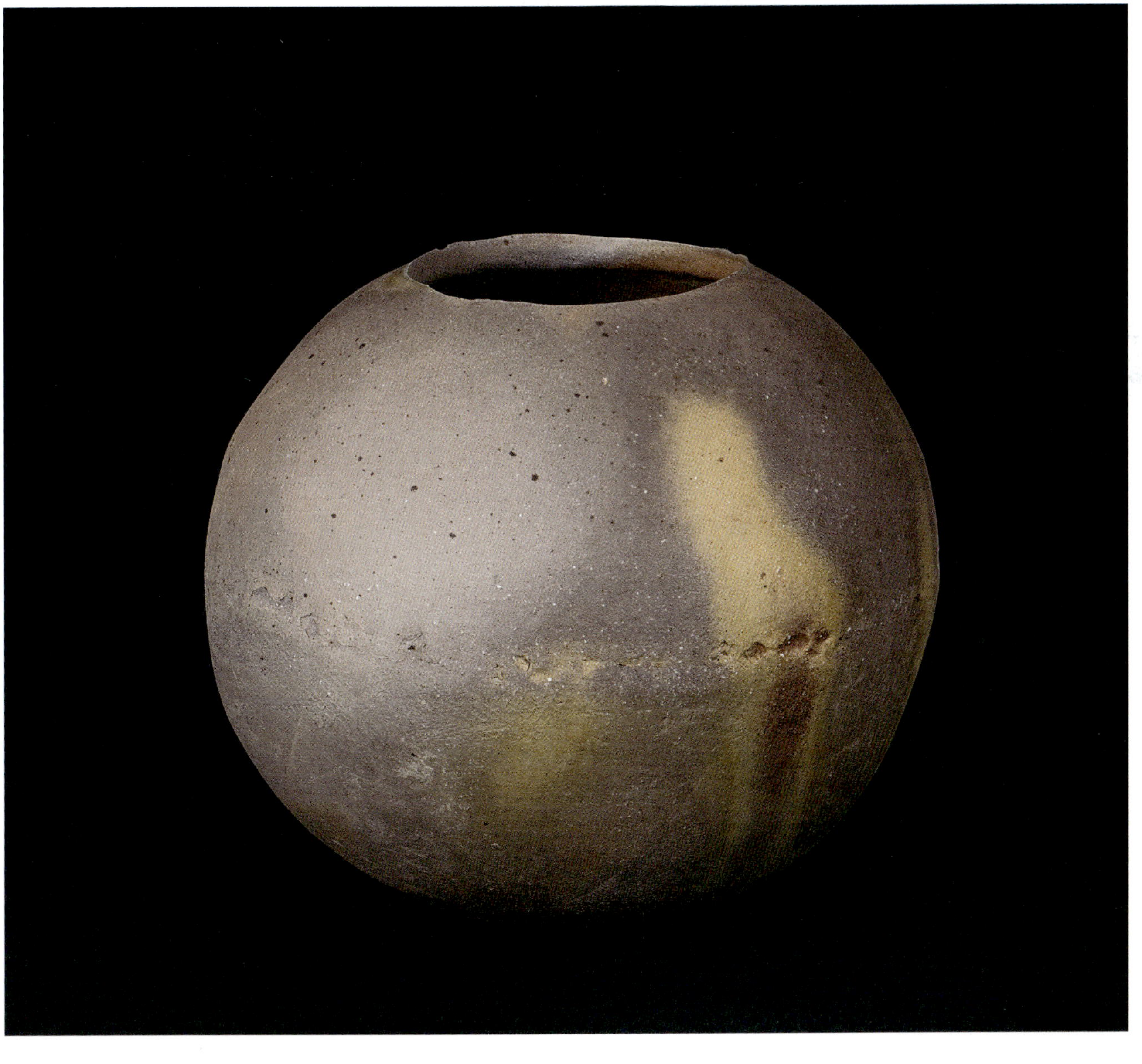

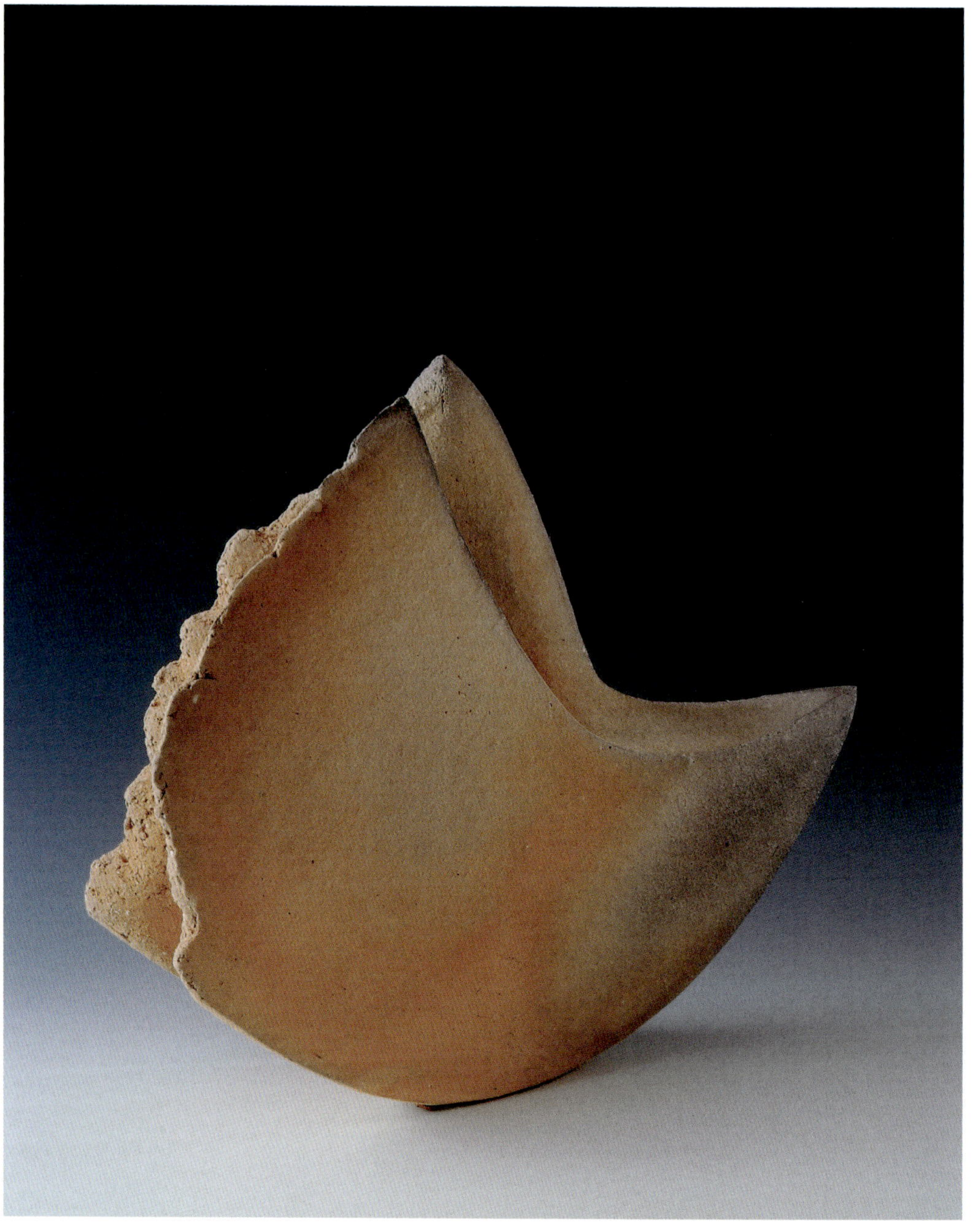

 TSUBASA, 2008 ······· 40 × 17 × 36 cm (15.7 × 6.7 × 14.1 inches) ······· Private Collection

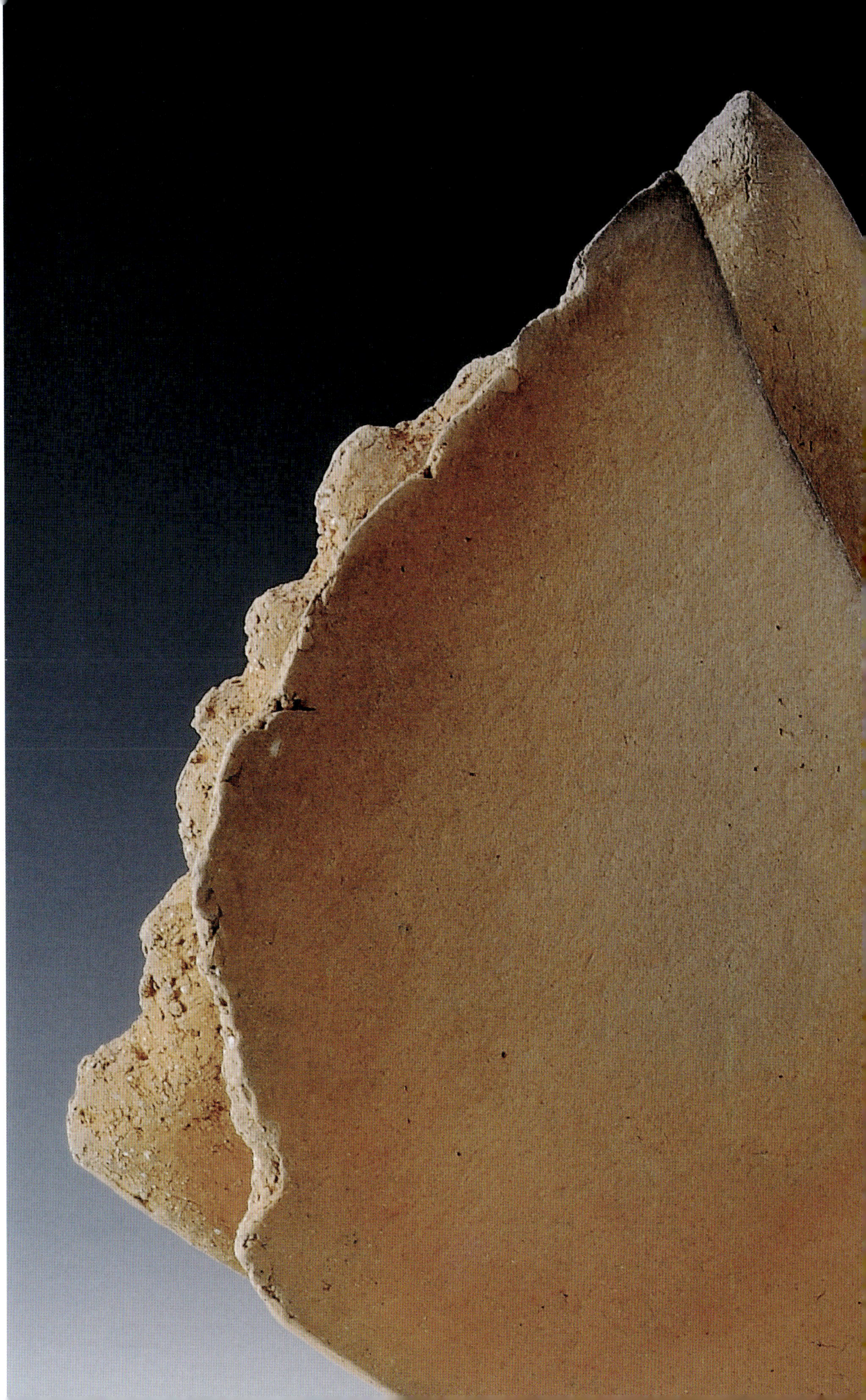

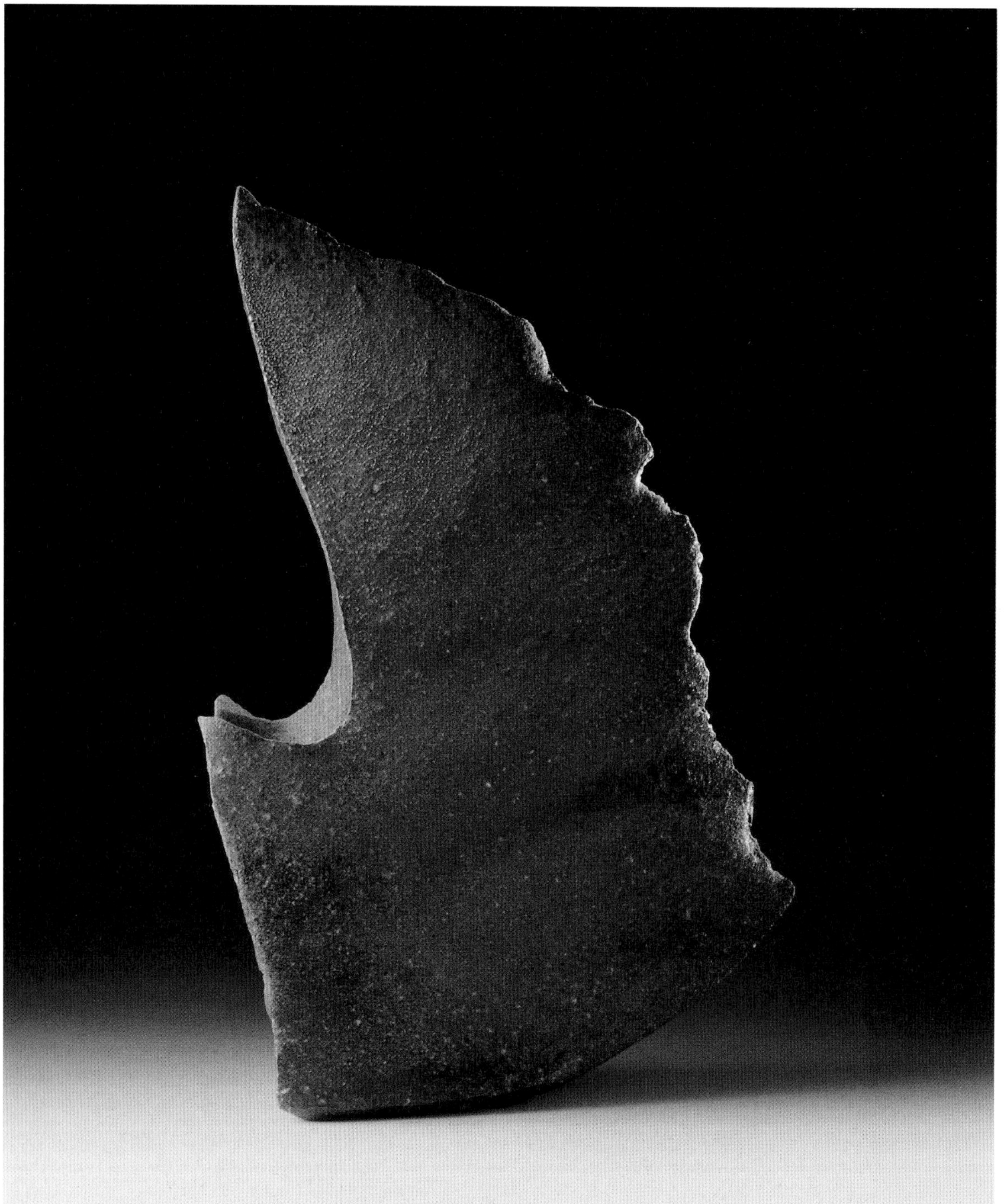

13 TSUBASA, 2008 ······· 25 × 13 × 39 cm (9.8 × 5.1 × 15.3 inches) ······· Collection of the artist
14 Slice of Earth, 1999 ······· 20 × 17 × 31 cm (7.9 × 6.7 × 12.2 inches) ······· Collection of the artist

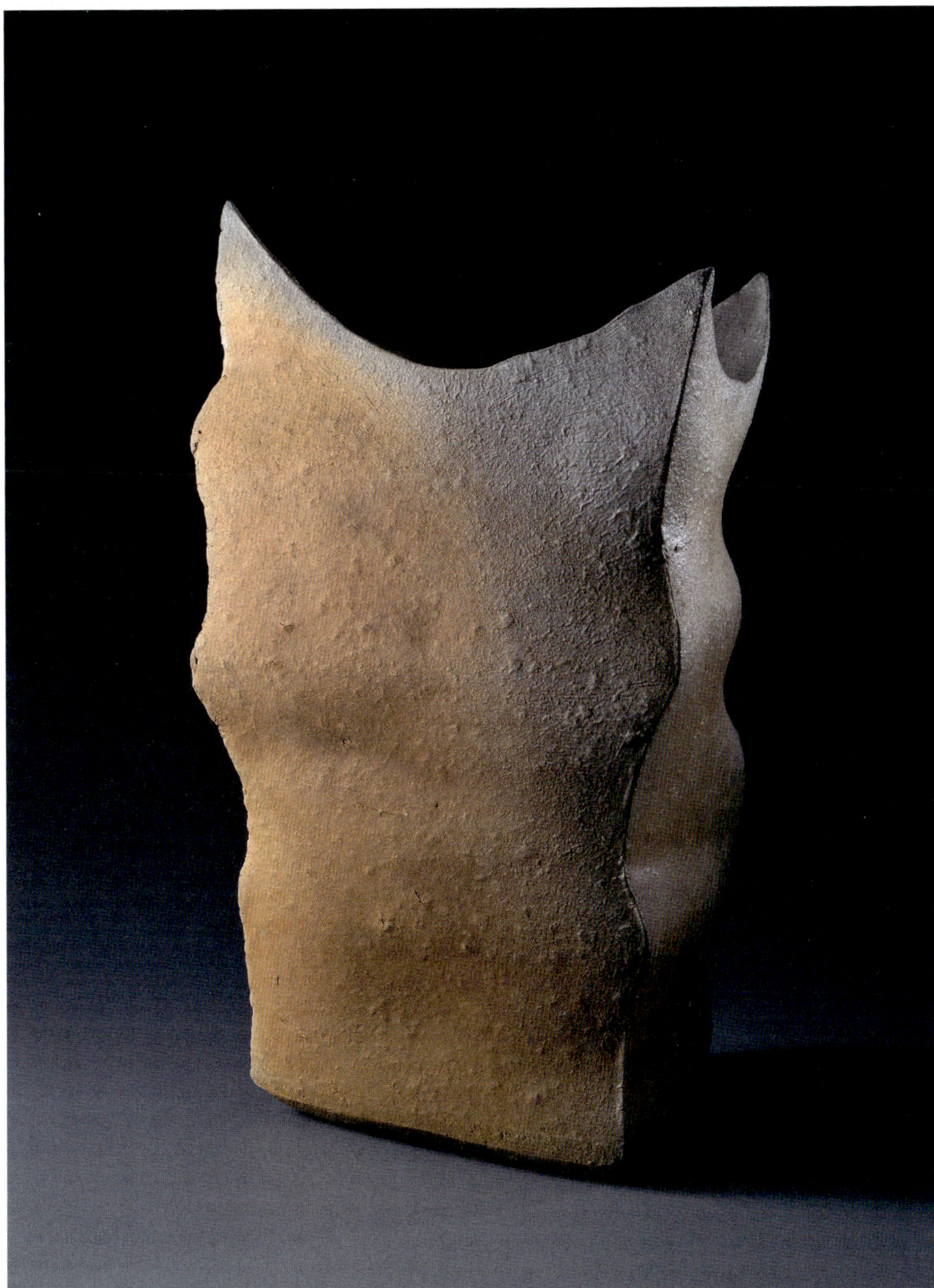

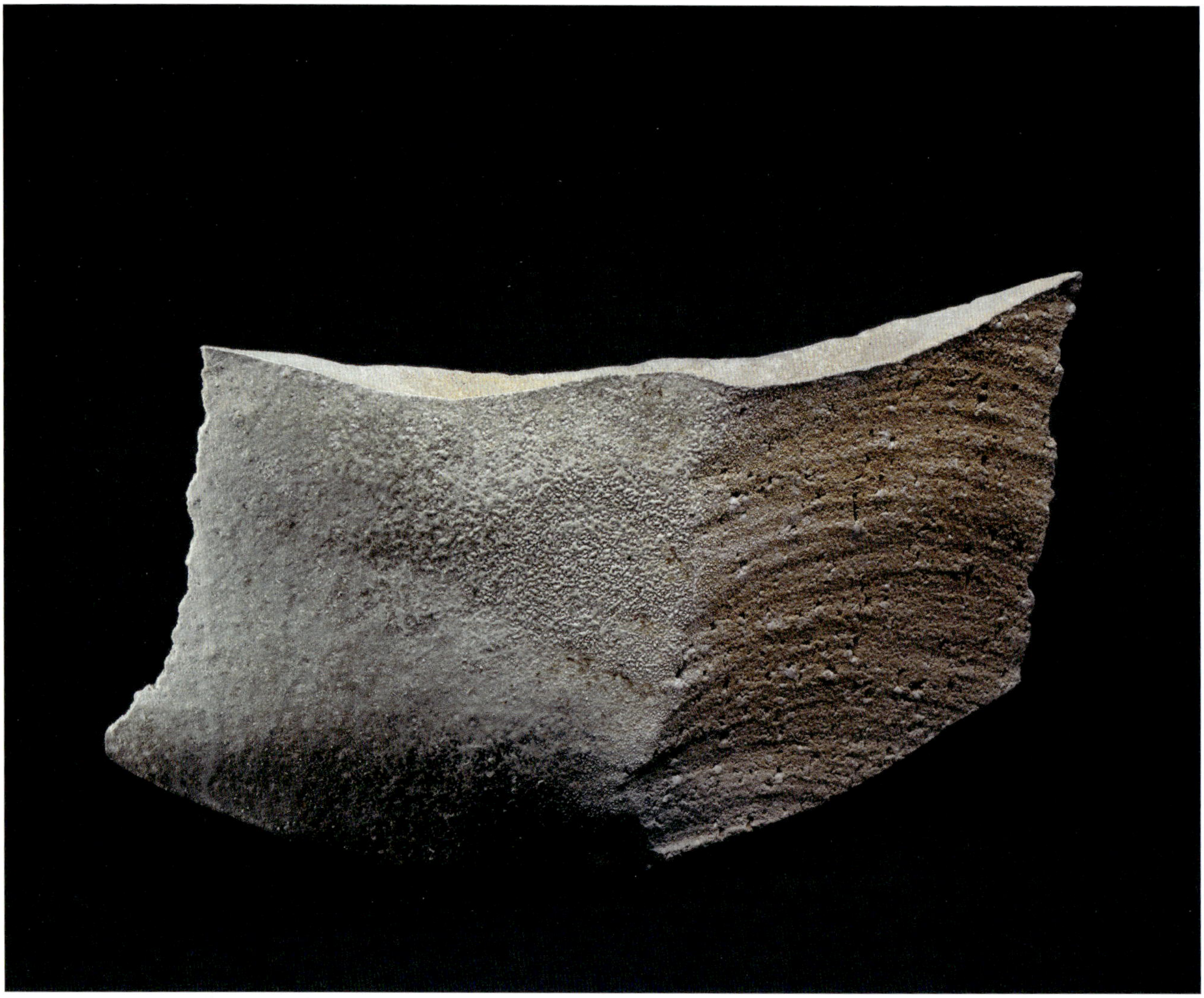

15 Slice of Earth, 1994 ······· 48 × 10 × 25.4 cm (18.9 × 3.9 × 10 inches) ······· Samuel and Gabrielle Lurie Collection, New York

16 TSUCHIKURE, 2010 ······· 19 × 10 × 17 cm, 15 × 10 × 15 cm (7.5 × 3.9 × 6.7 inches, 5.9 × 3.9 × 5.9 inches) ······· Collection of the artist

17 Slice of Earth, 2011 ······· 40 × 10 × 22.5 cm (15.7 × 3.9 × 8.6 inches) ······· Collection of the artist

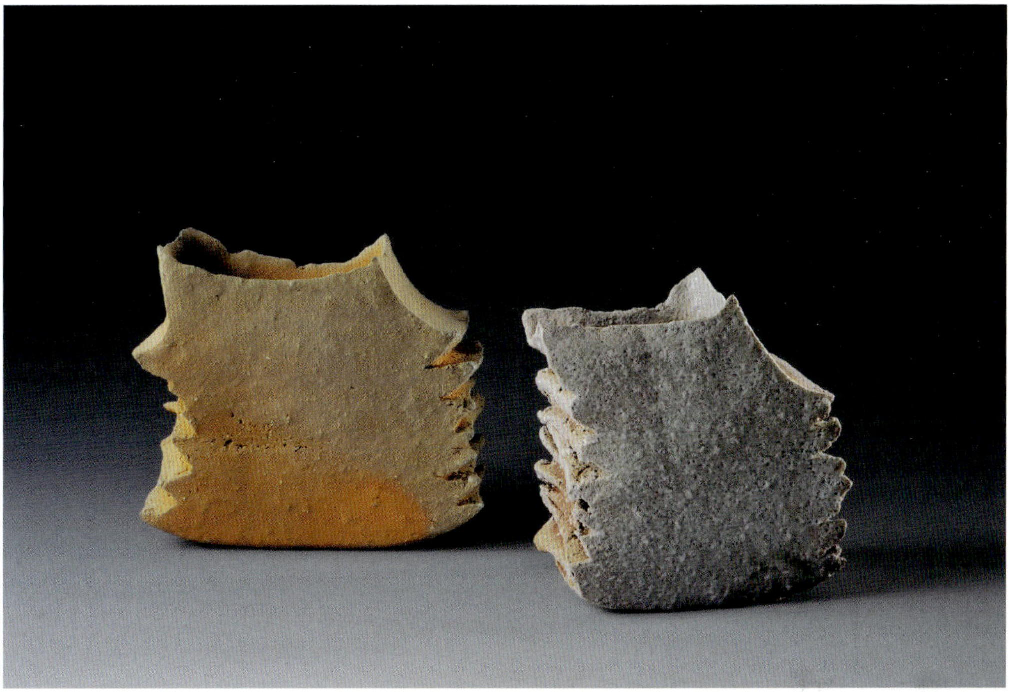

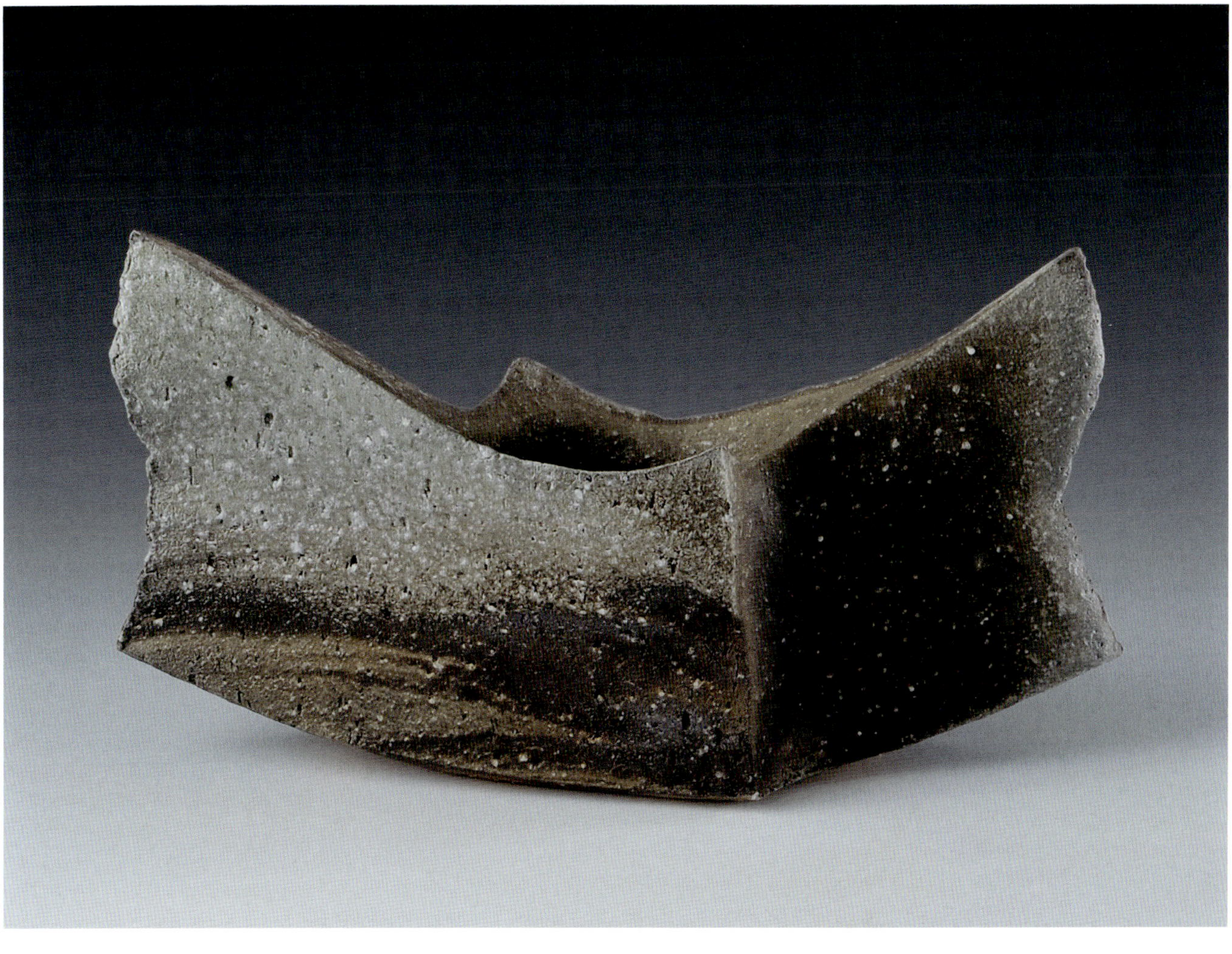

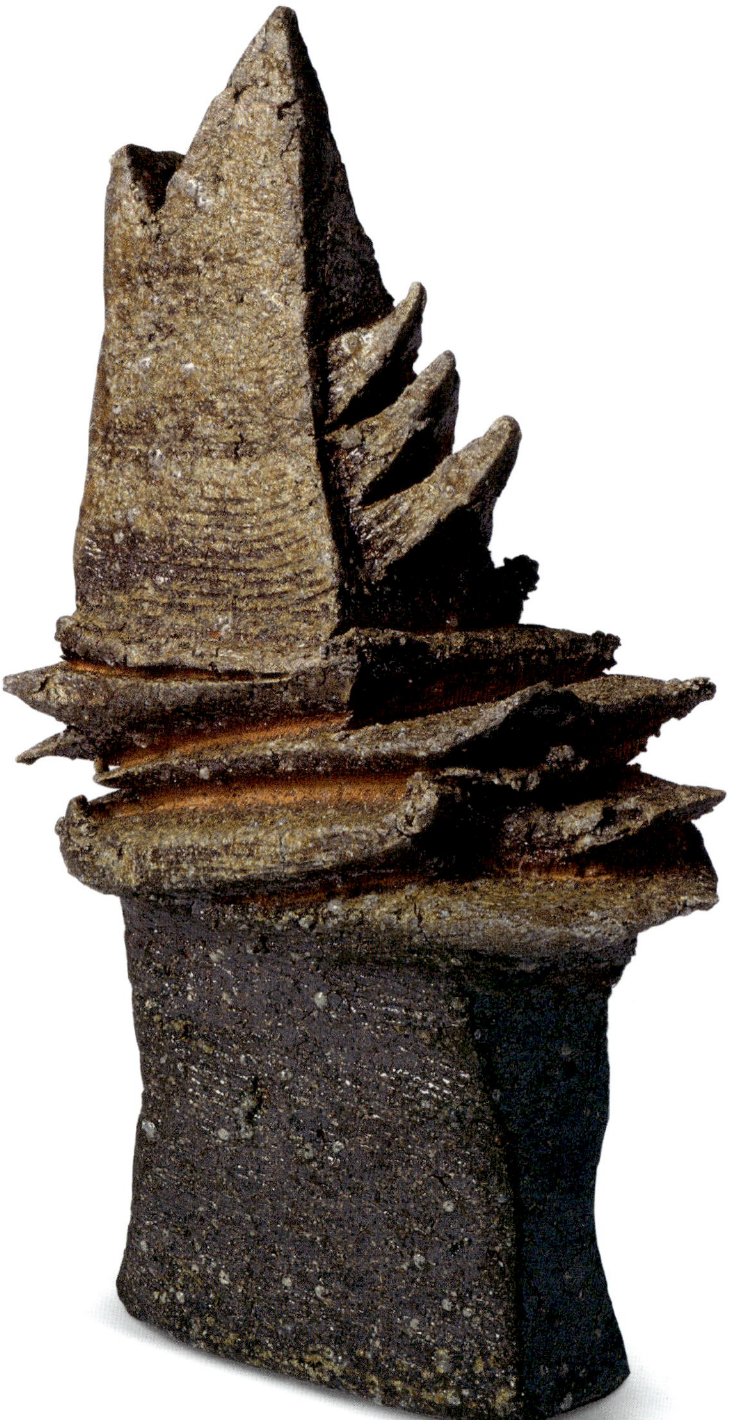

18 Slice of Earth in Australia, 2004 ······· 15 × 16 × 31 cm (5.9 × 6.3 × 12.2 inches) ······· Collection of the artist

19 Alpaca in Australia, 2004 ······· 29 × 23 × 30 cm (11.4 × 9.0 × 11.8 inches) ······· Collection of the artist

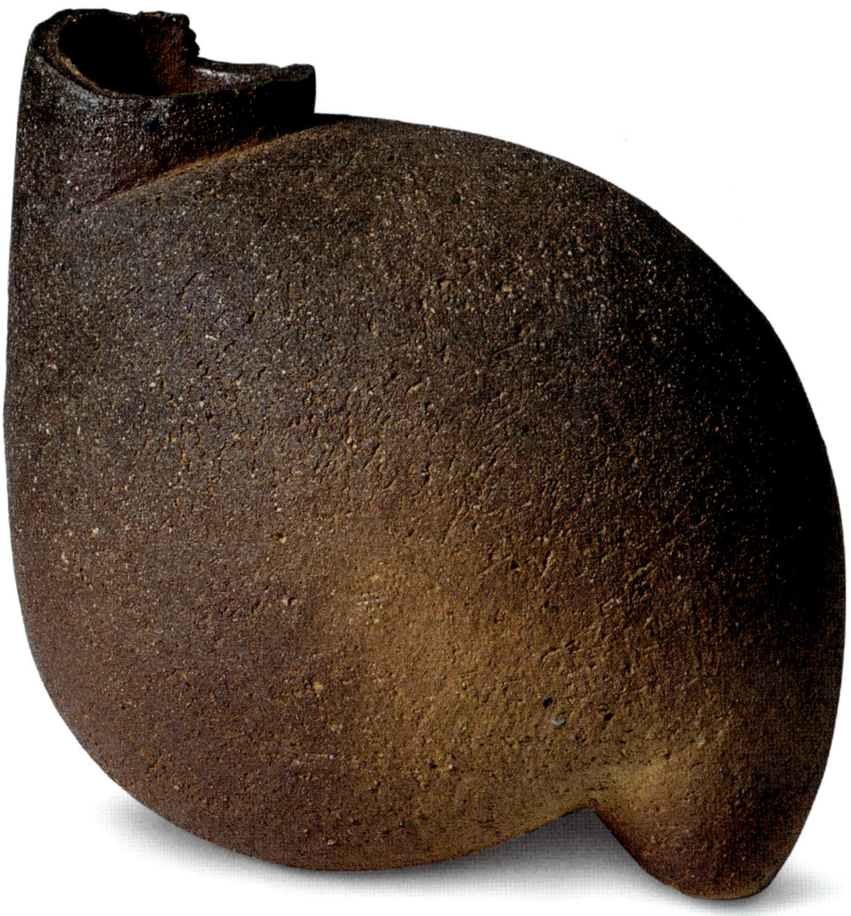

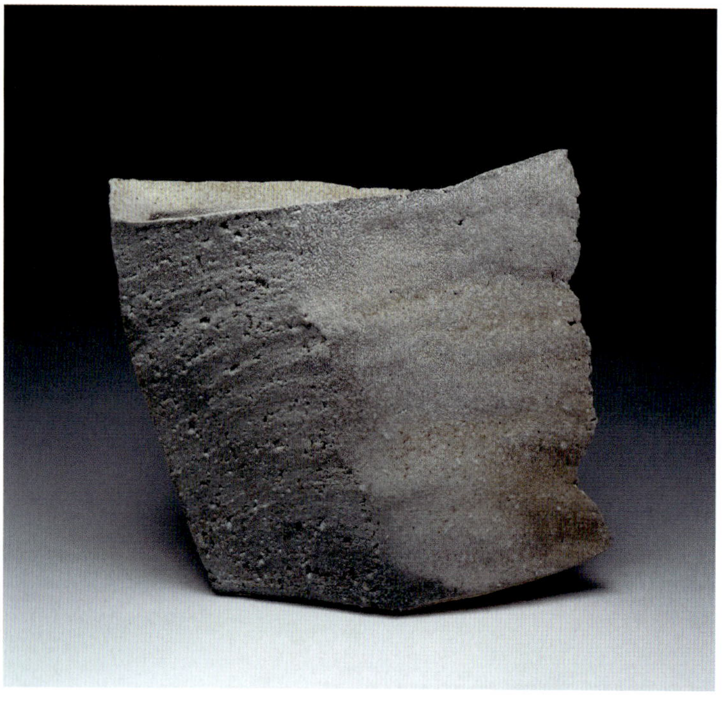

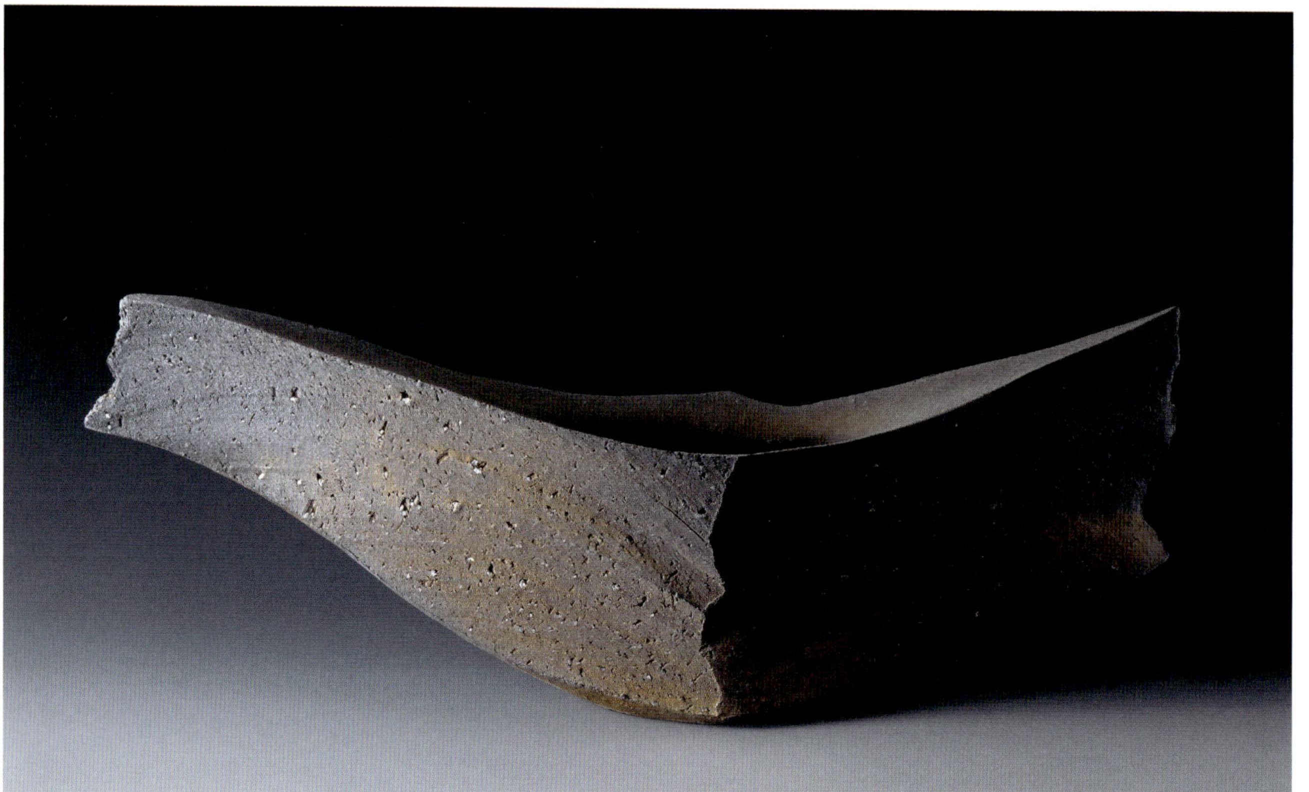

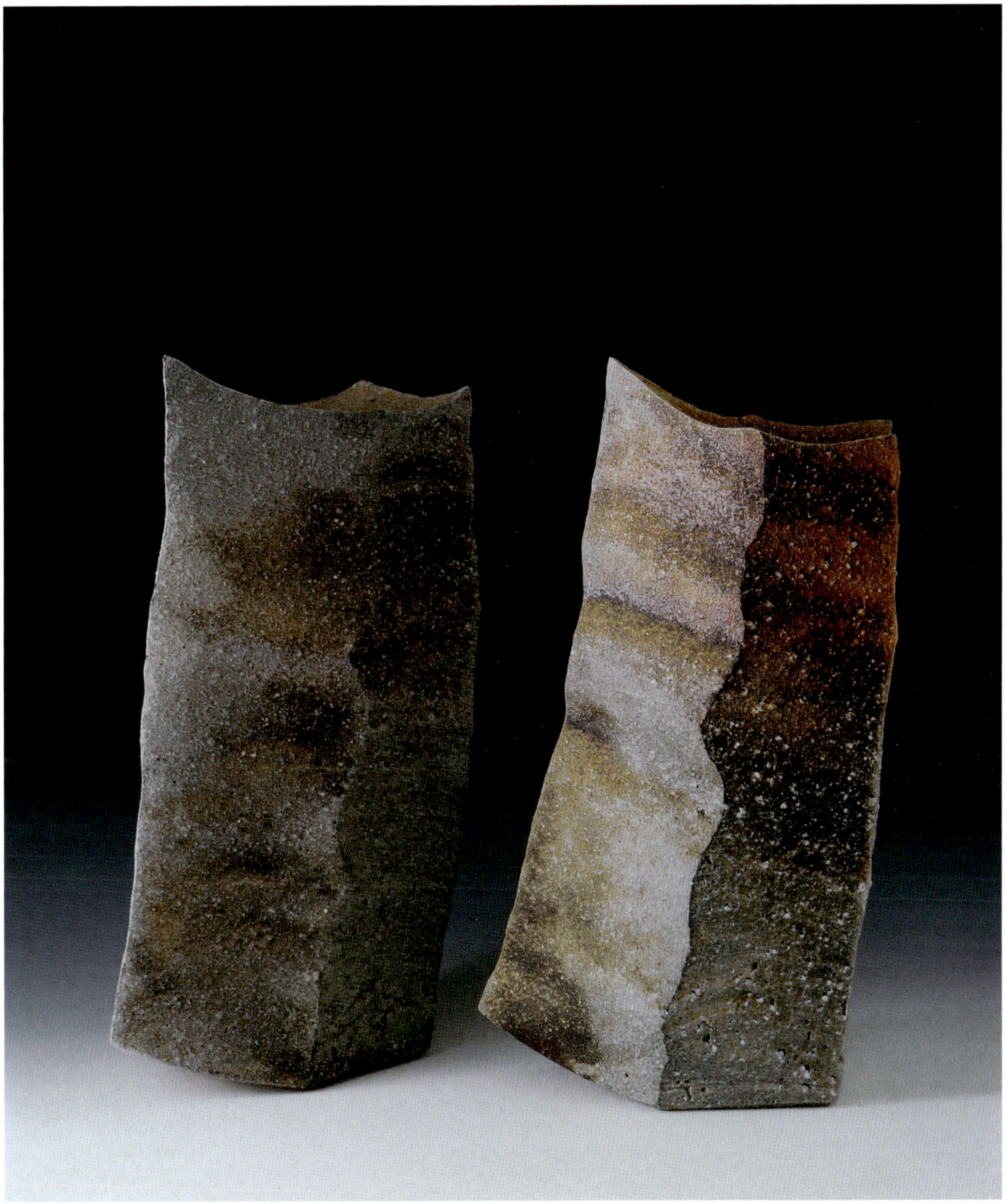

20 Slice of Earth, 1999 ······· 38 × 15 × 33 cm (14.5 × 5.9 × 13.0 inches) ······· The Gardiner Museum of Ceramic Art, Toronto

21 Impression in Form, 2002 ······· 76 × 16 × 29.2 cm (29.9 × 6.3 × 11.4 inches) ······· Philadelphia Museum of Art, Philadelphia

22 KAZE, 2007 ······· 27 × 16 × 49.6 cm, 29 × 16 × 48.5 cm (10.6 × 6.3 × 19.5 inches, 11.4 × 6.3 × 19.0 inches) ······· Private Collection

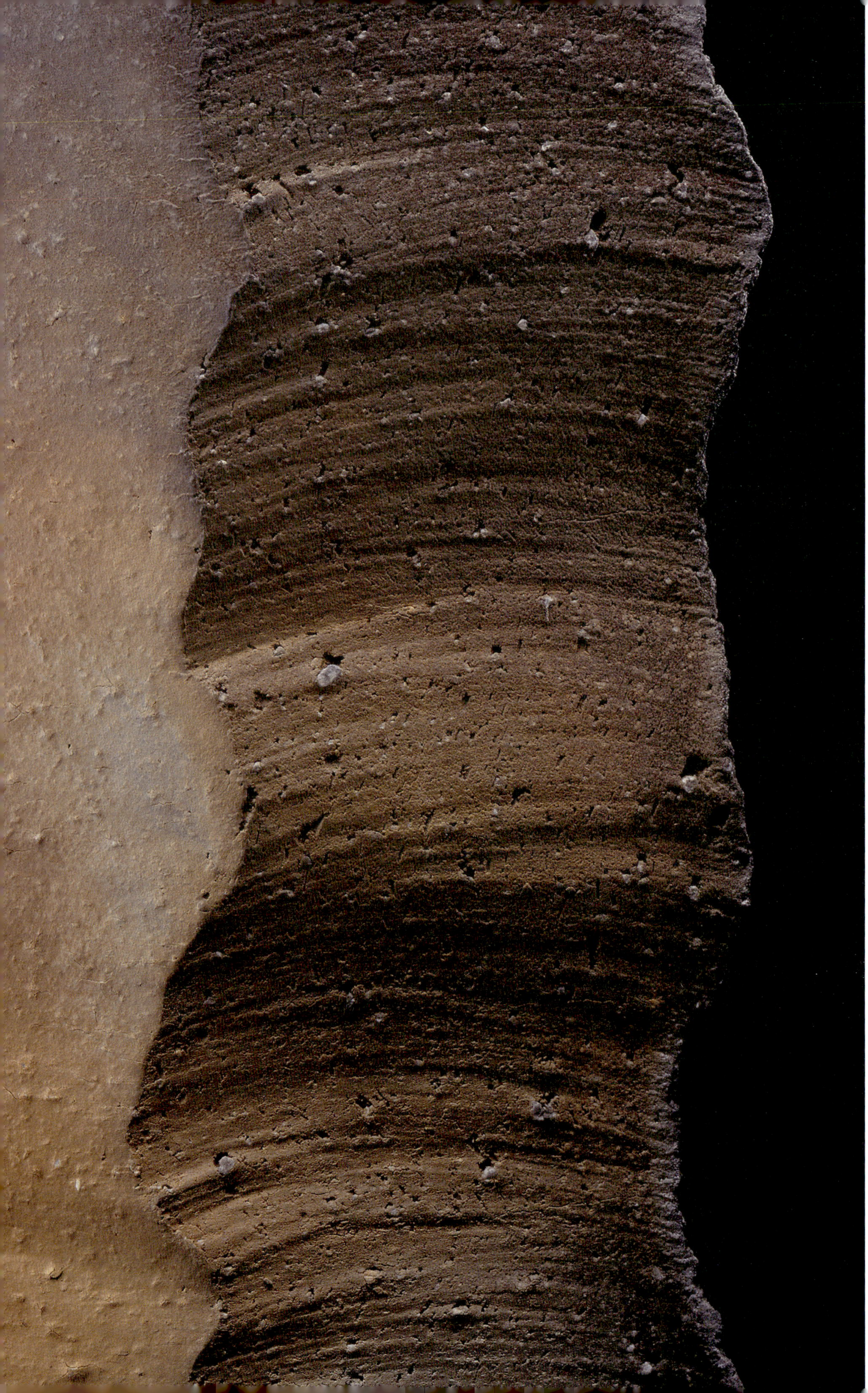

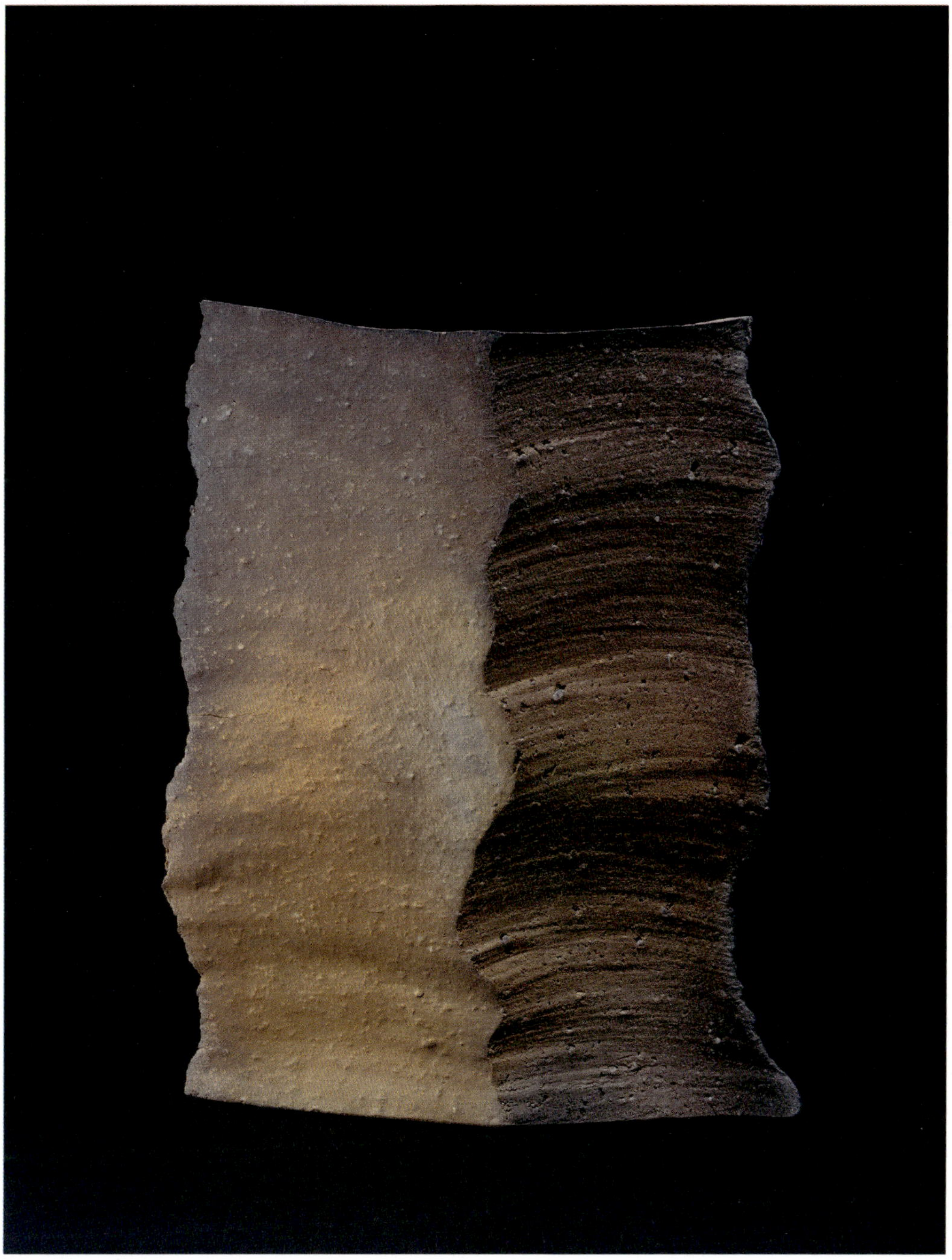

23 Slice of Earth, 1996 ······· 40 × 14 × 53 cm (15.7 × 5.5 × 20.8 inches) ······· Collection of the artist

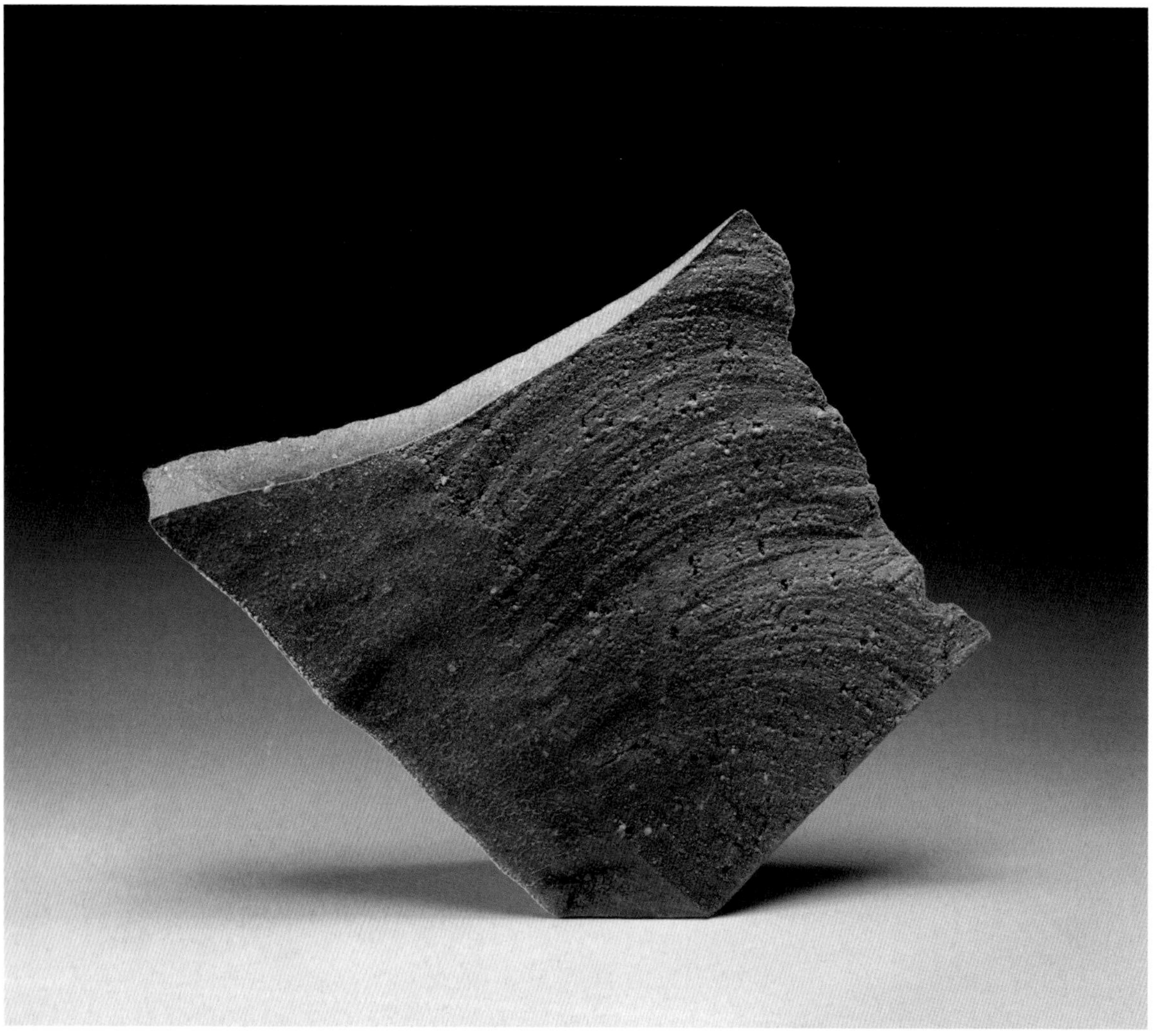

24 KAZE, 1994 ······· 47.4 × 10.8 × 39.0 cm (18.7 × 4.25 × 15.3 inches) ······· Private Collection

25 KAZE, 2001 ······· 44.9 × 14.9 × 50.8 cm (17.6 × 5.9 × 20 inches) ······· Museum of Arts and Design, New York

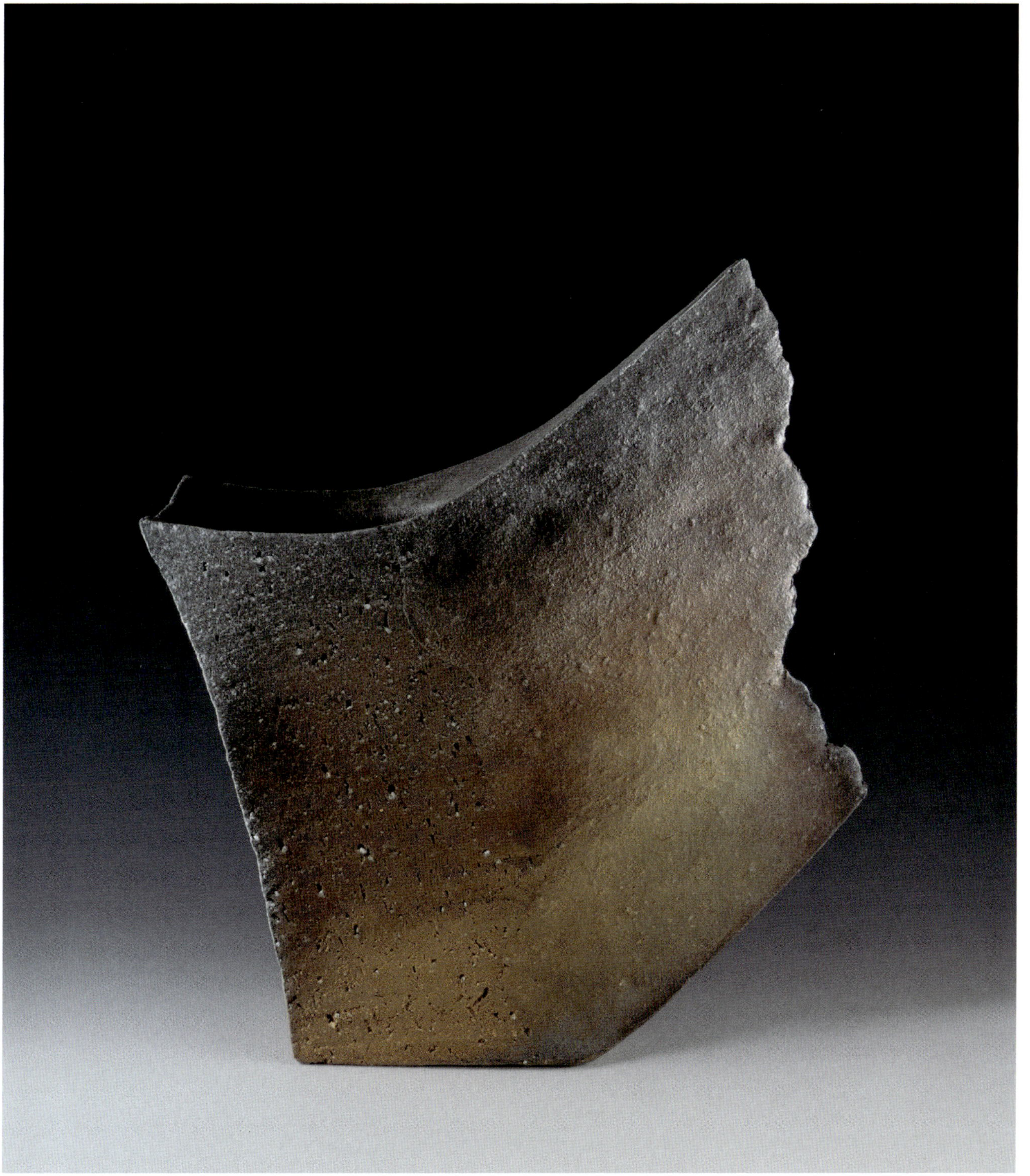

26 KAZE, 2004 ······· 54.6 × 8.9 × 49.5 cm (21.4 × 3.5 × 19.4 inches) ······· Gift of Halsey and Alice North, The Metropolitan Museum of Art, New York

27 KAZE, 2002 ······· 36.2 × 10.8 × 47.0 cm (14.2 × 4.2 × 18.5 inches) ······· Private Collection

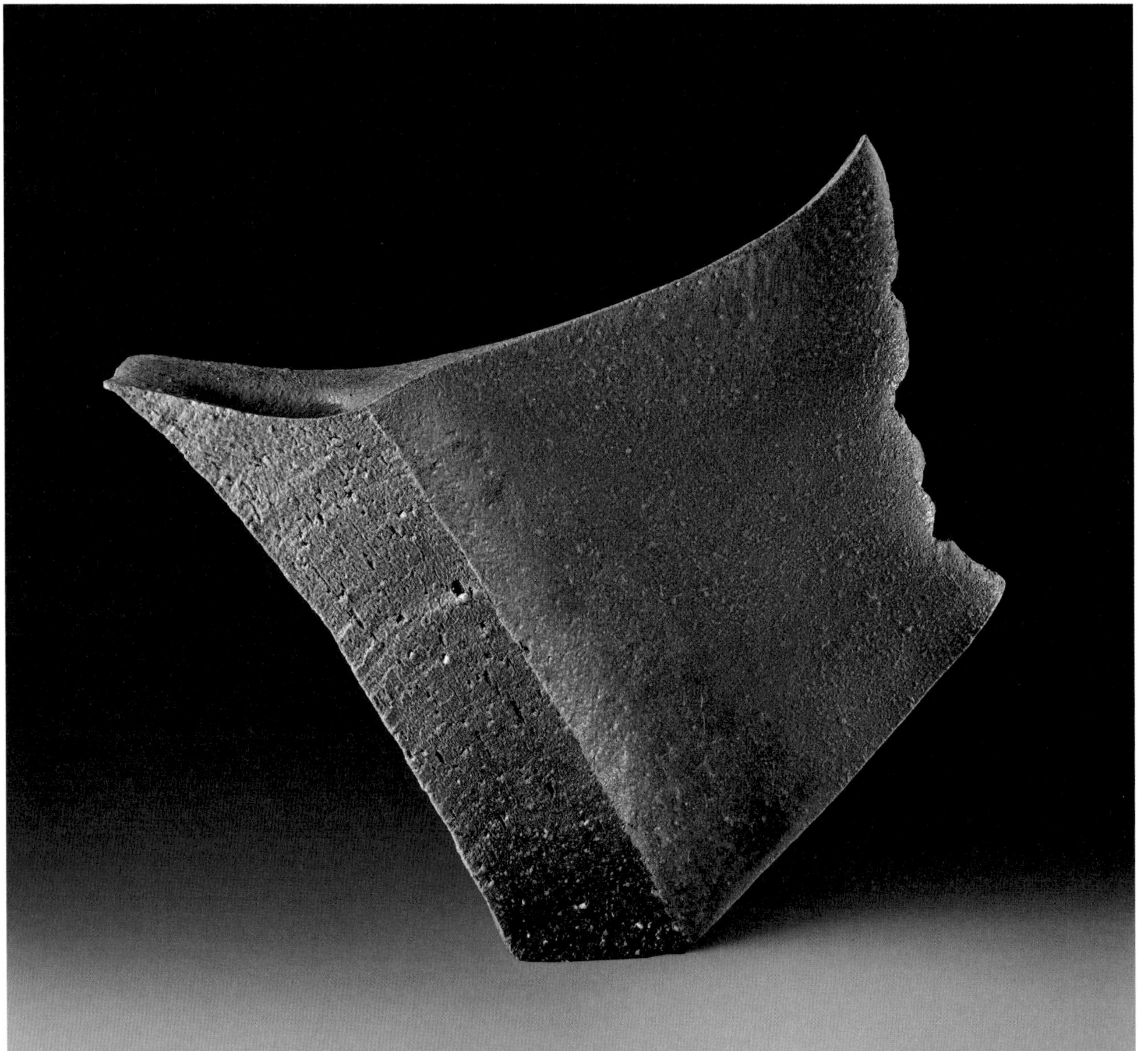

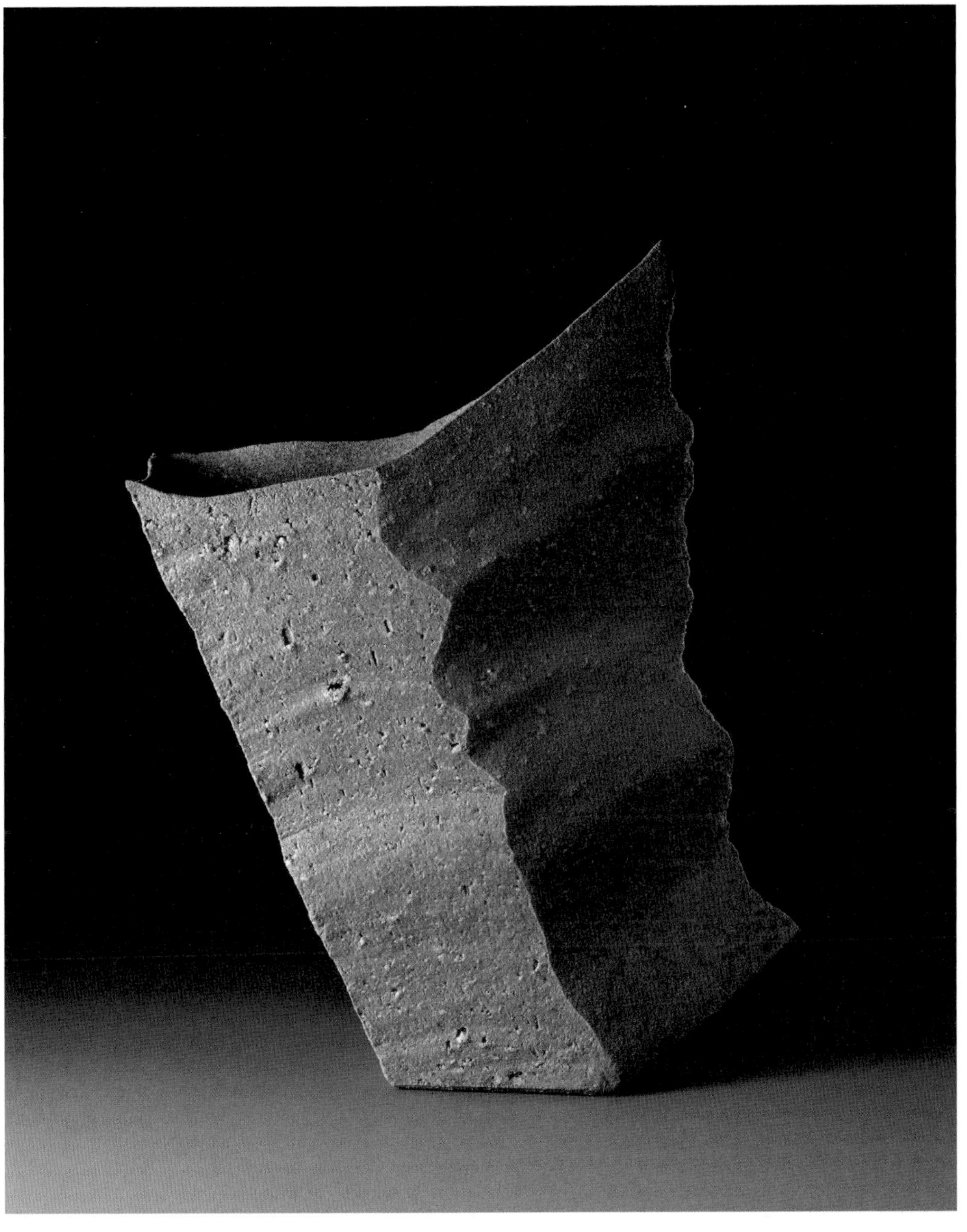

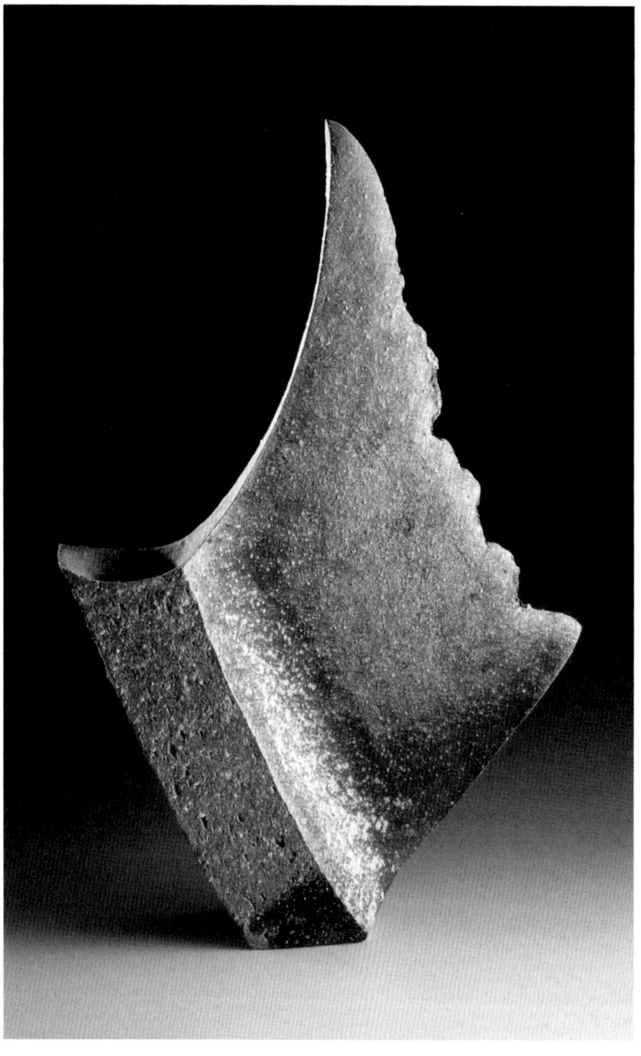

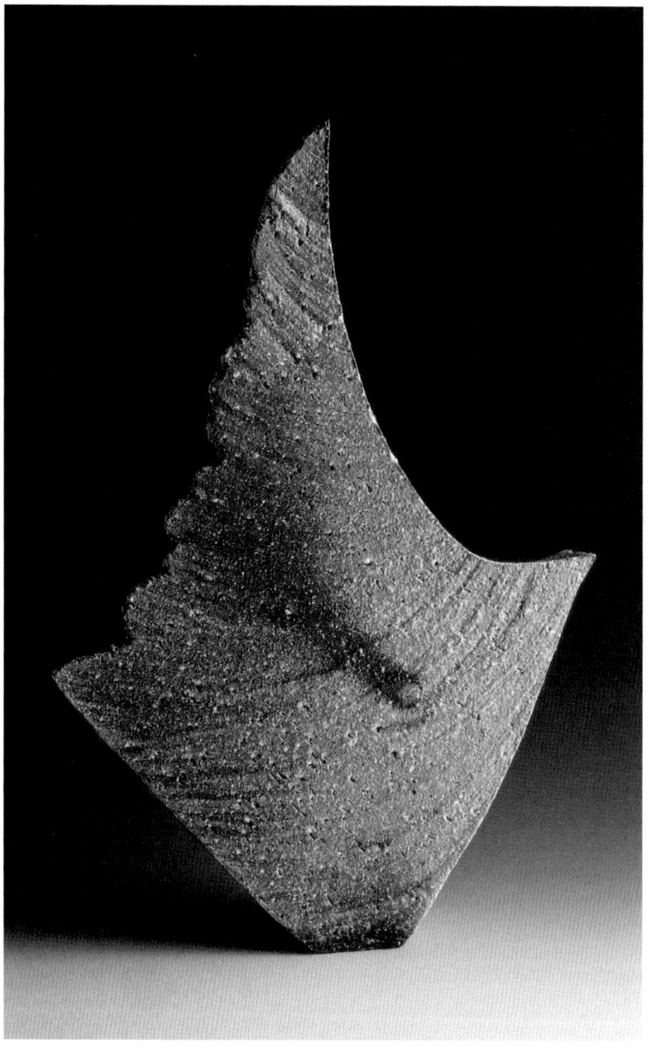

28 KAZE, 2006 (front and back view) ······· 54.5 × 15.5 × 67.0 cm (21.4 × 6.1 × 26.3 inches) ······· Private Collection

29 KAZE, 2007 ······· 38.5 × 12.0 × 63.0 cm (15.1 × 4.72 × 24.8 inches) ······· Collection of the artist

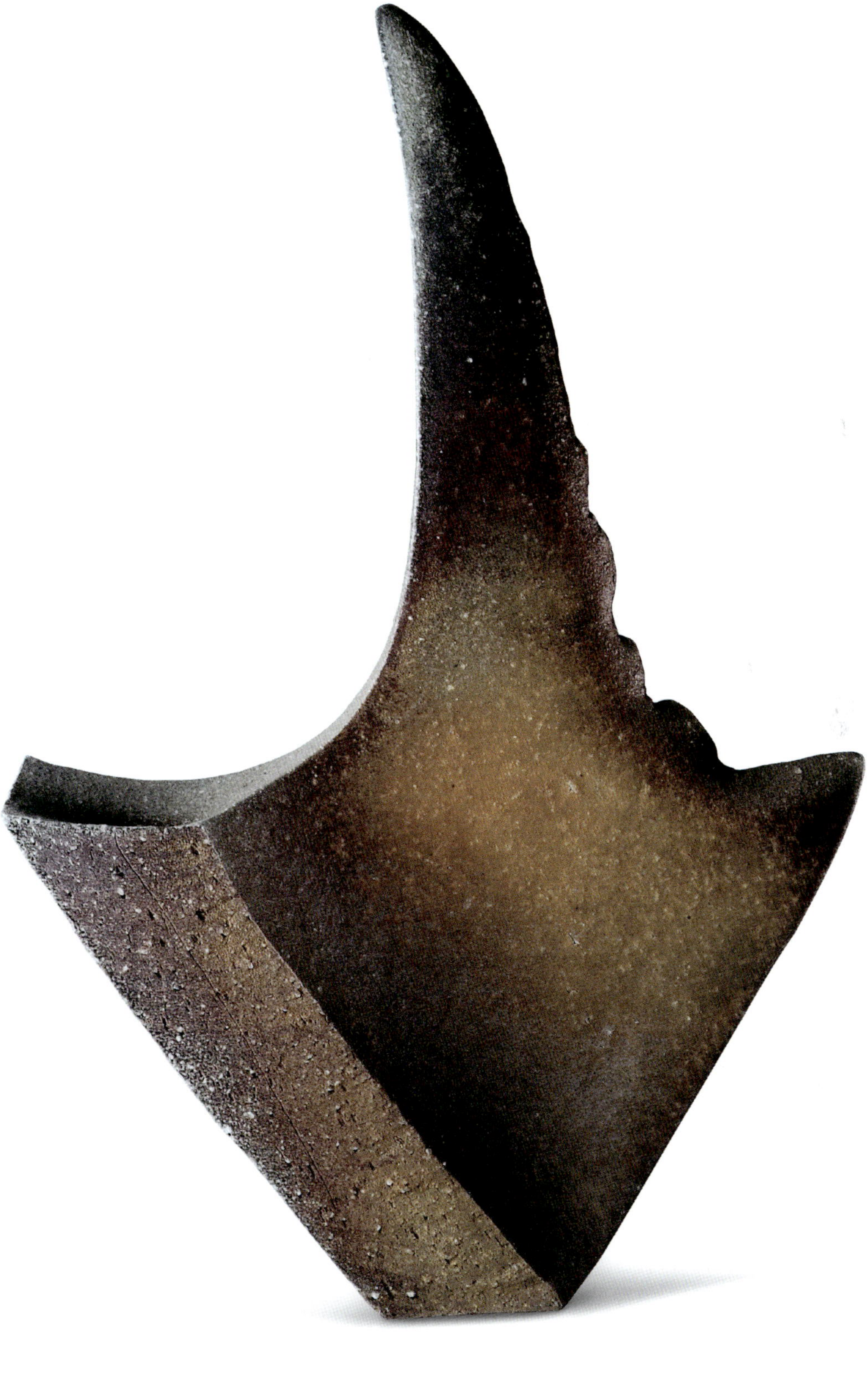

30 Untitled, 1991 ······· 46 × 10 × 30 cm (18.1 × 3.9 × 11.8 inches) ······· Collection of the artist

31 DANPEN, 2011 ······· 23 × 14 × 41 cm (9.0 × 5.5 × 16.1 inches) ······· Collection of the artist

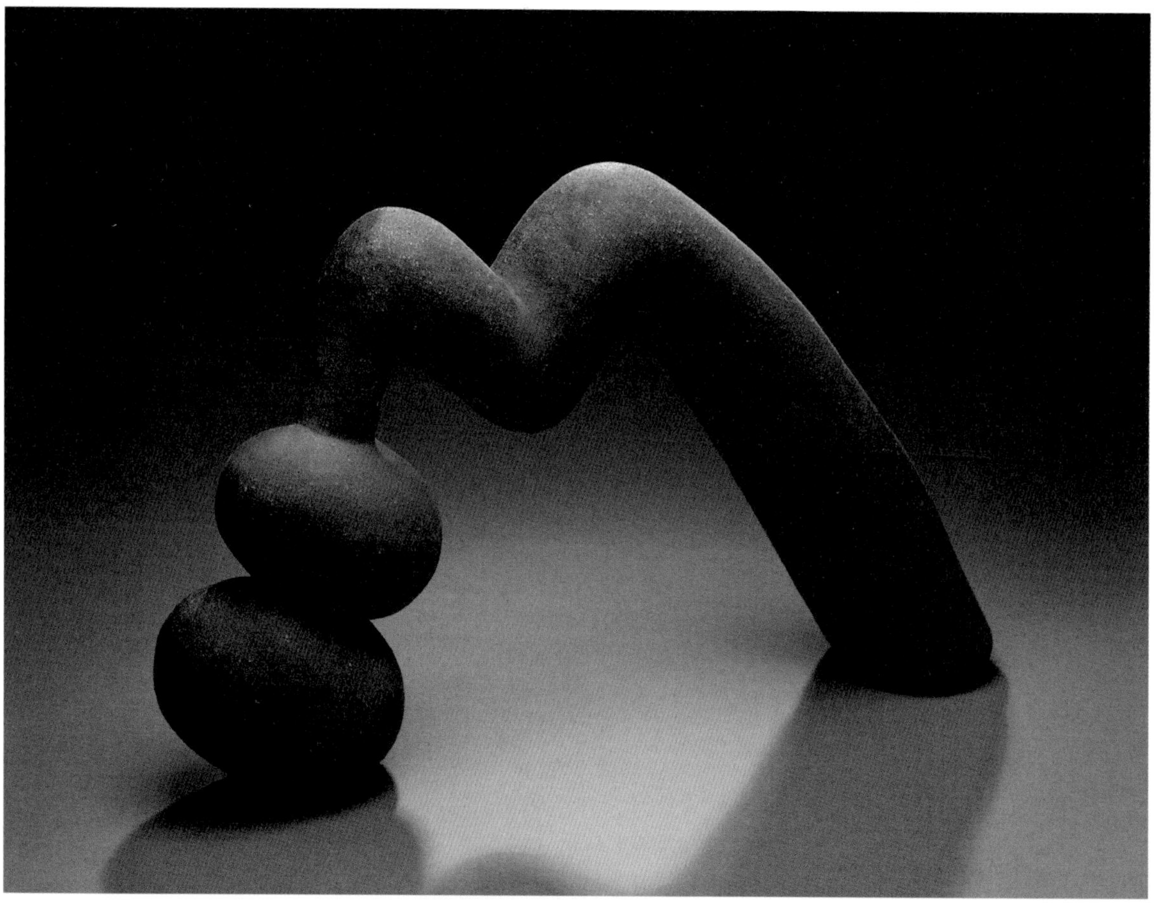

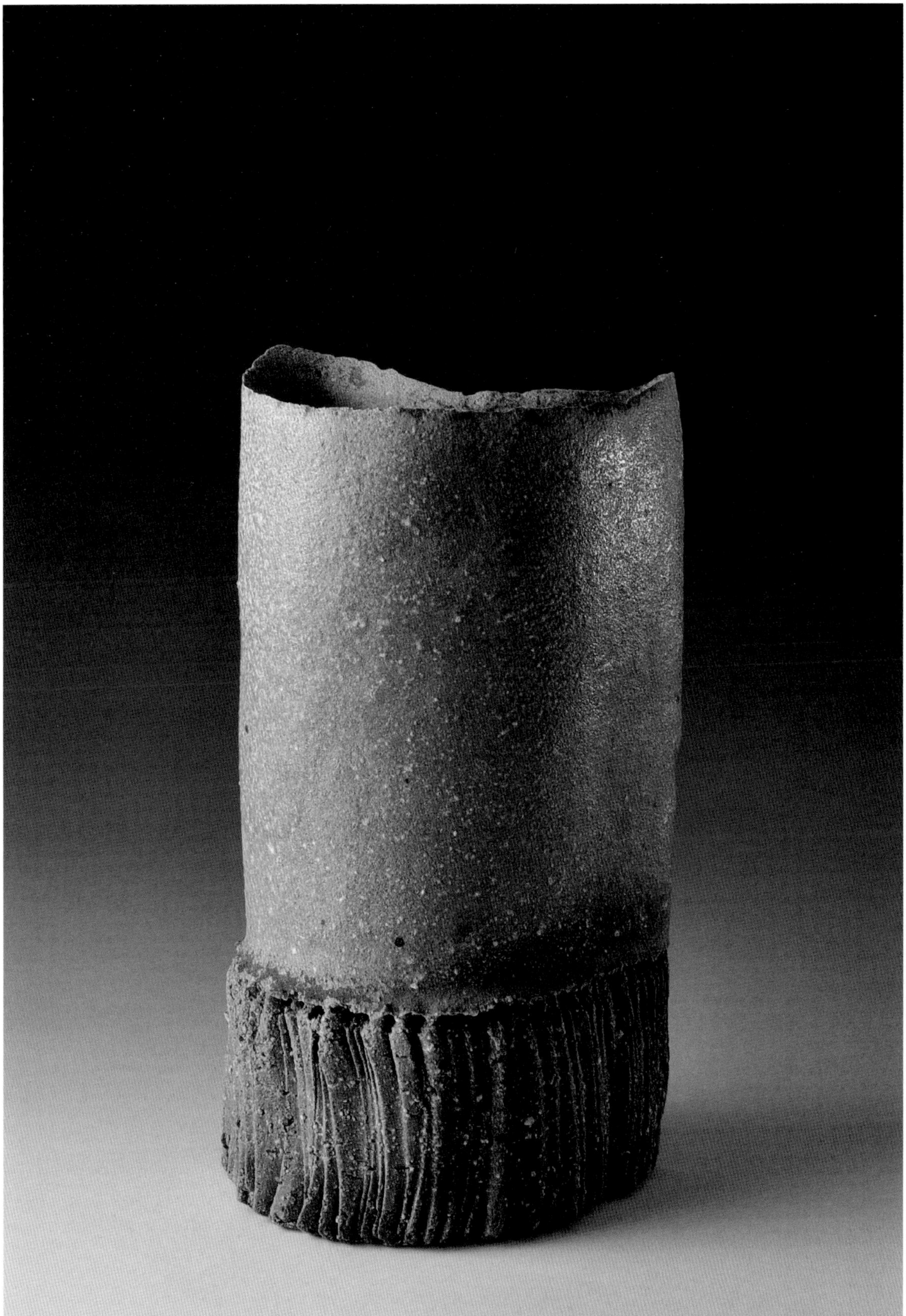

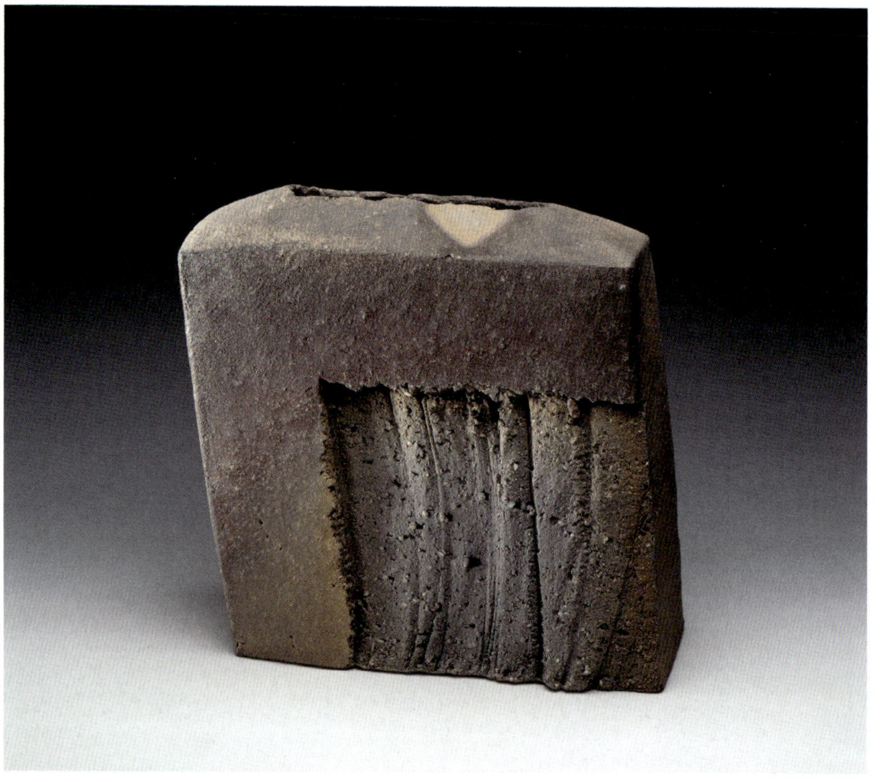

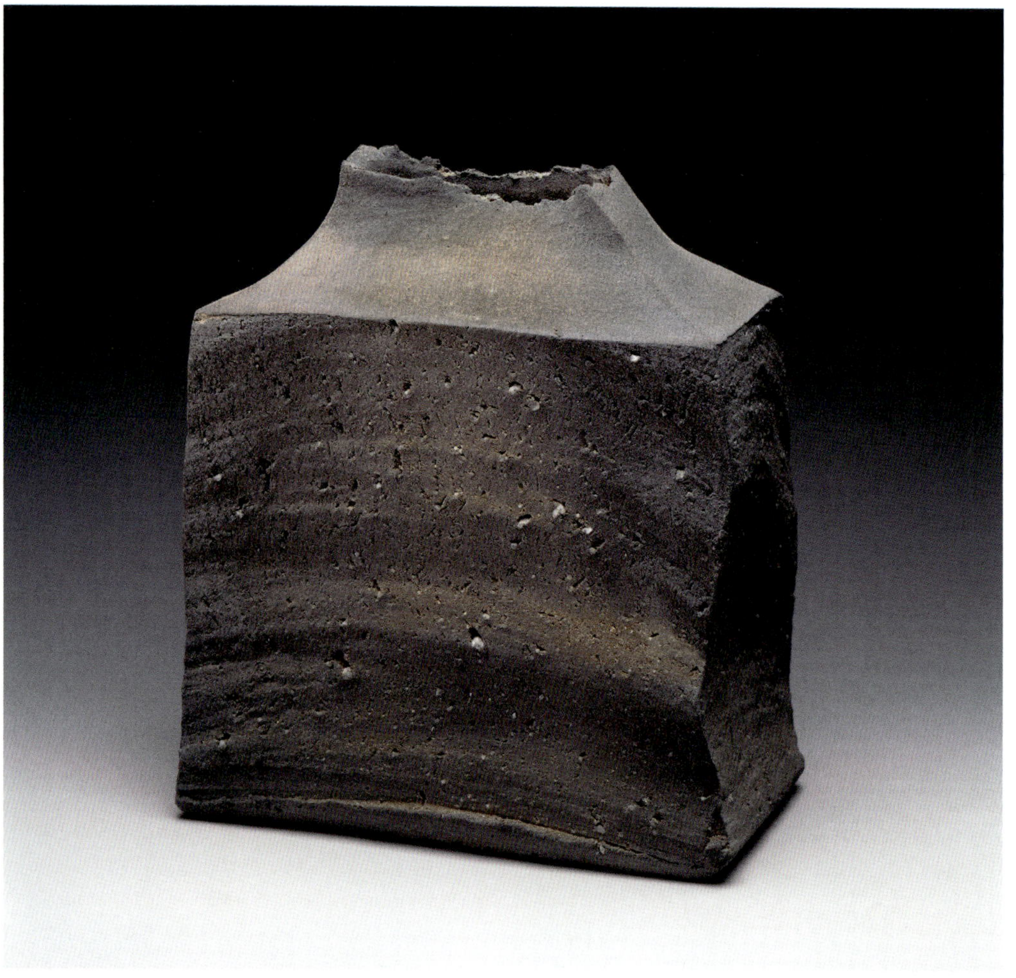

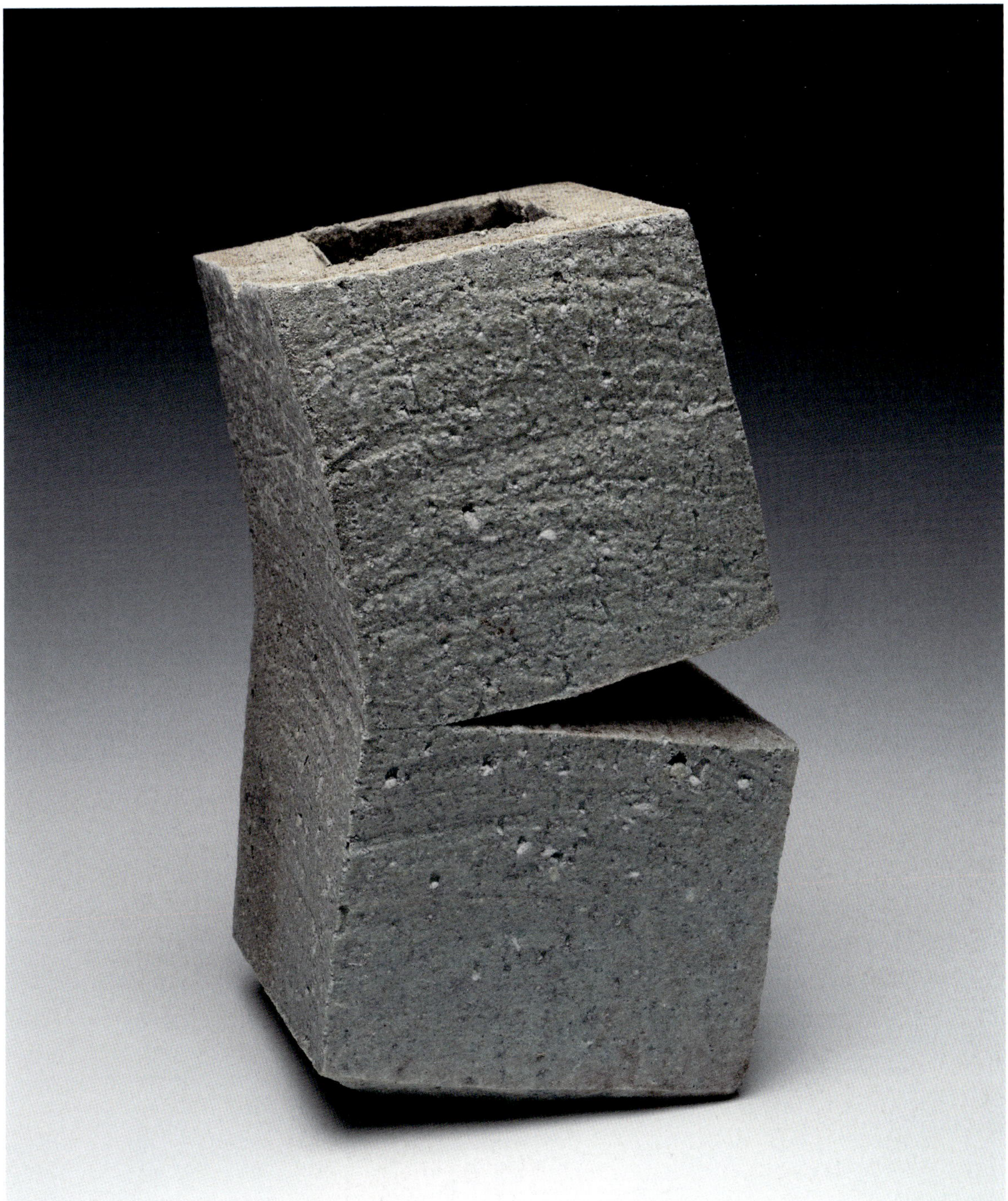

32 Untitled, 1992 ······· 25 × 9 × 22.5 cm (9.8 × 3.5 × 8.6 inches) ······· Private Collection
33 Shigaraki Shizenyu MENTORI Vase, 1992 ······· 24.5 × 13 × 28 cm (9.6 × 5.1 × 11.0 inches) ······· Museum für Kunst und Gewerbe Hamburg
34 Shigaraki Shizenyu MENTORI Vase, 1988 ······· 15 × 18 × 28 cm (5.9 × 7.0 × 11.0 inches) ······· Collection of the artist

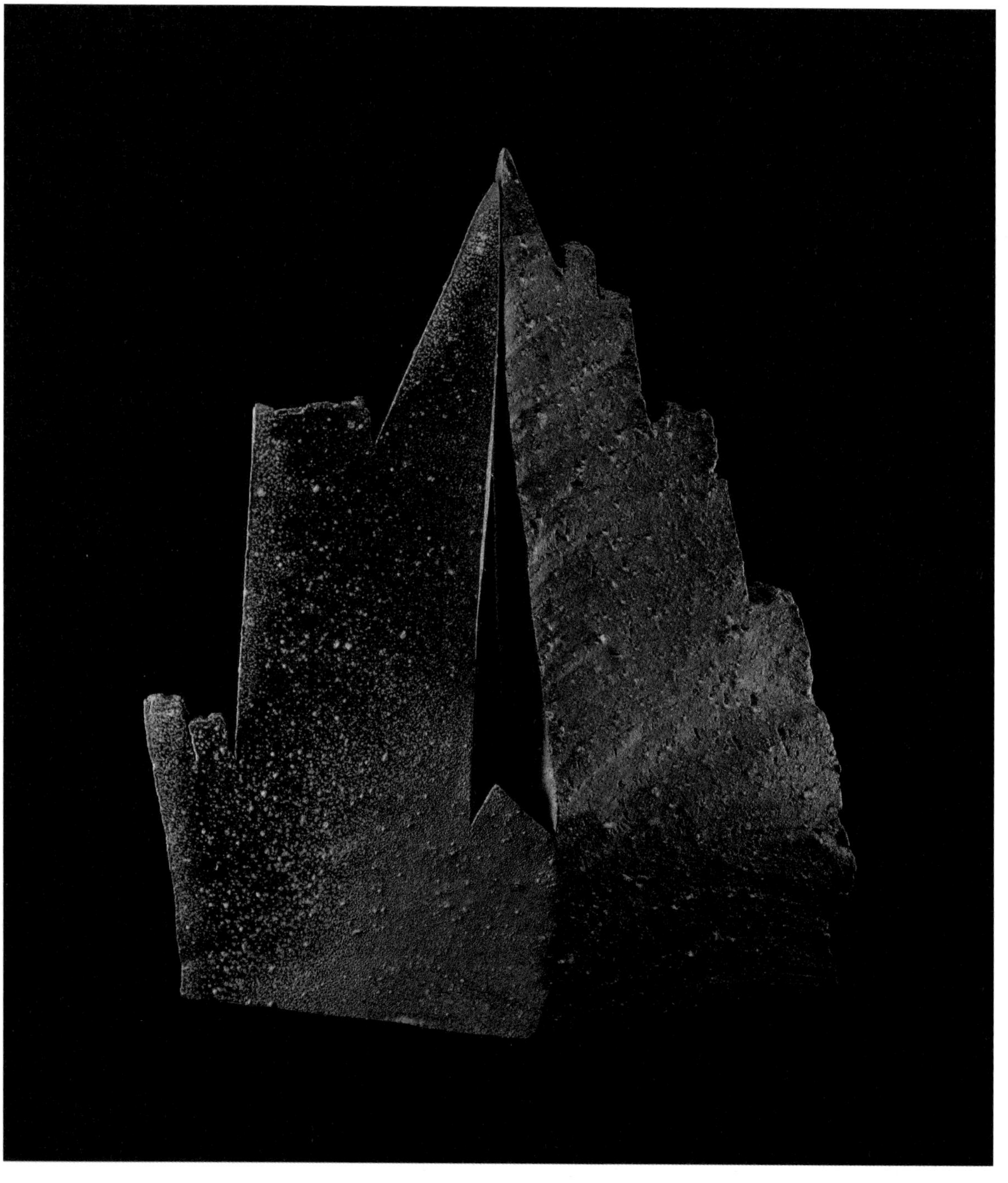

35 Impression in Form, 1997 ······· 37 × 8 × 47 cm (14.5 × 3.1 × 18.5 inches) ······· Samuel and Gabrielle Lurie Collection, New York

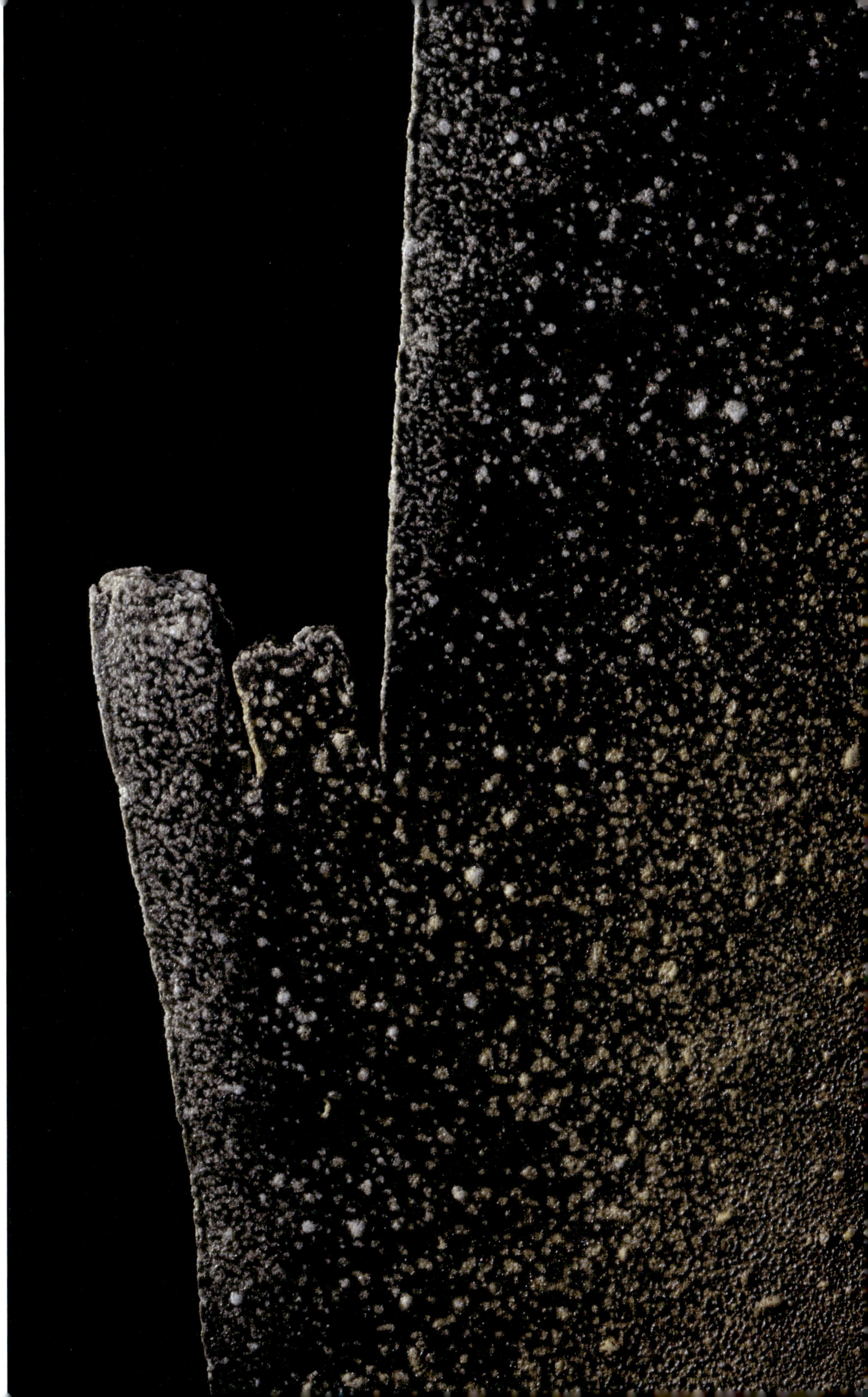

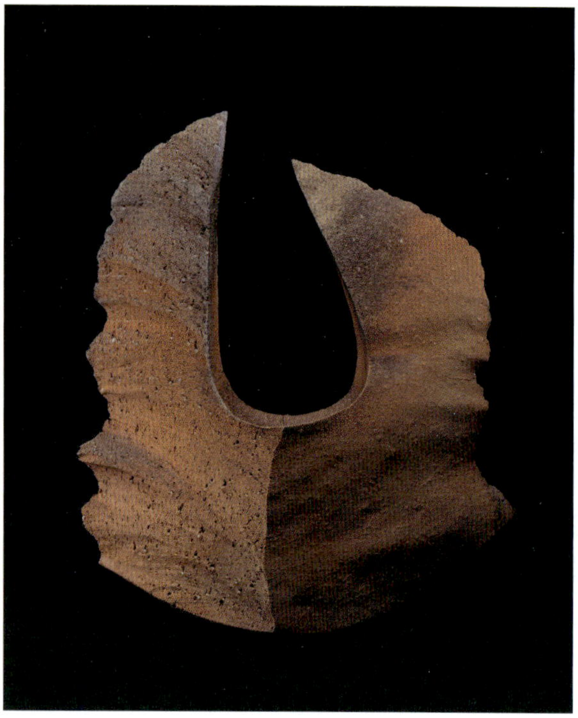

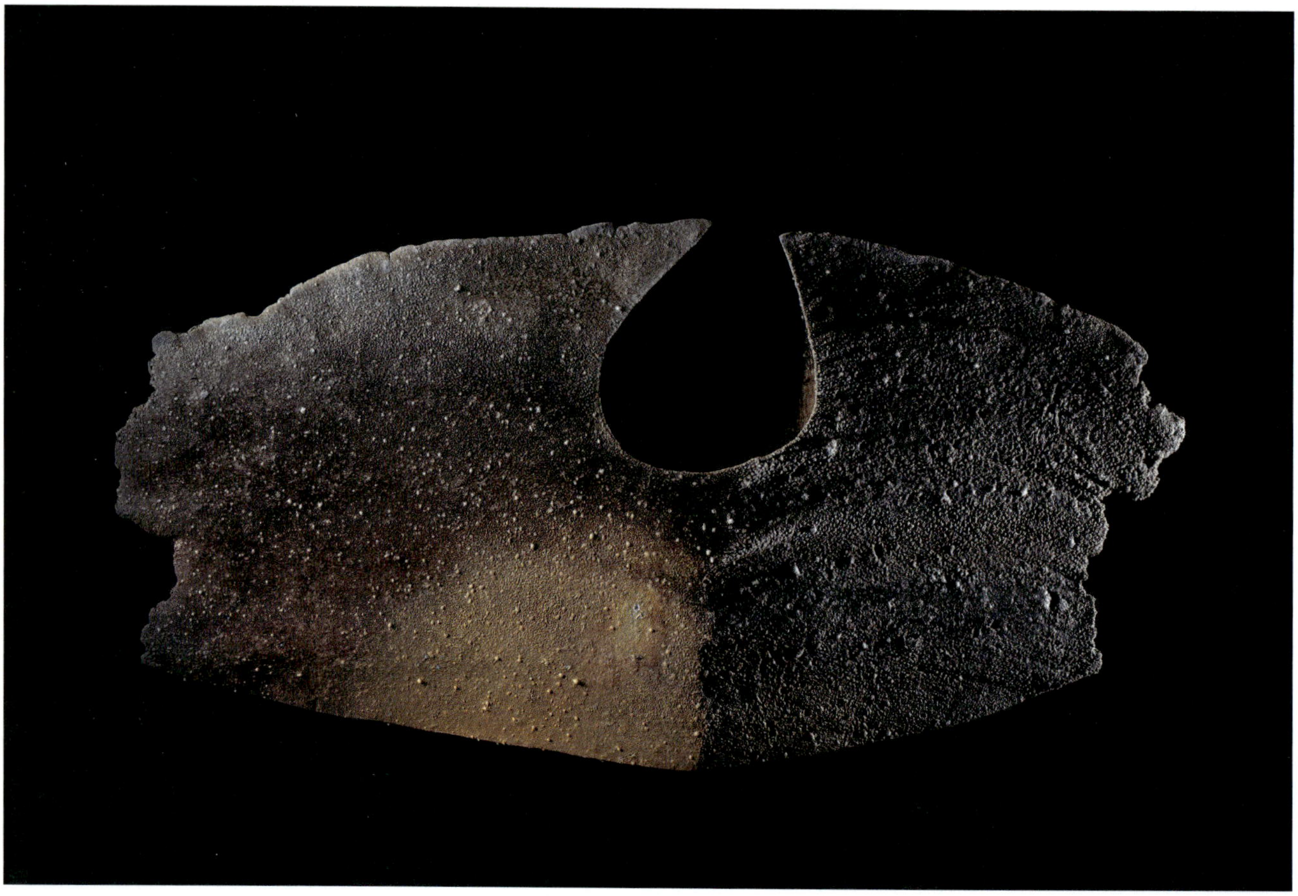

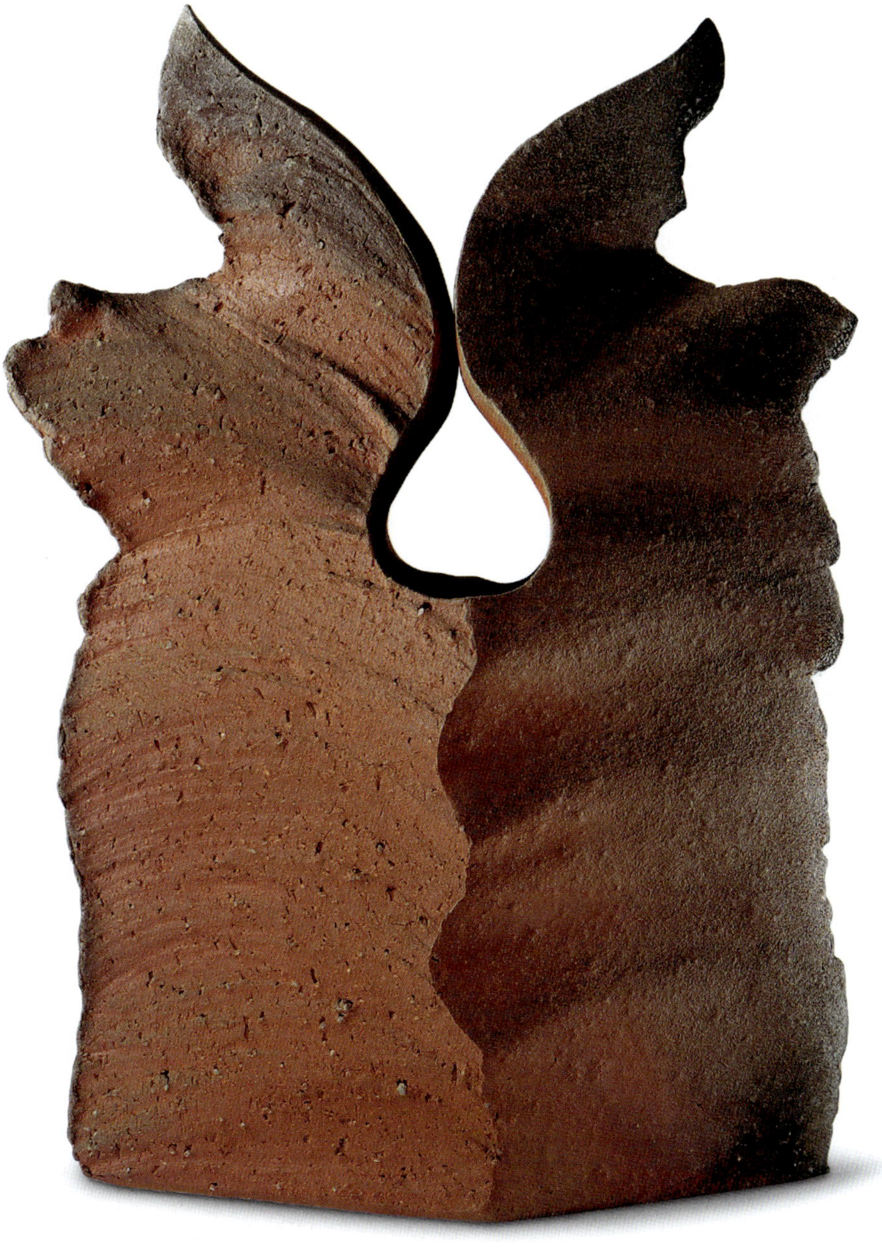

36 Impression in Form, 1999 ······· 53.5 × 16.8 × 52.7 cm (21.1 × 6.6 × 20.7 inches) ······· Samuel and Gabrielle Lurie Collection, New York

37 Impression in Form, 1997 ······· 70 × 12 × 35 cm (27.6 × 4.7 × 13.8 inches) ······· Private Collection

38 HOMURA, 2011 ······· 43 × 13 × 61 cm (16.9 × 5.1 × 24.0 inches) ······· Collection of the artist

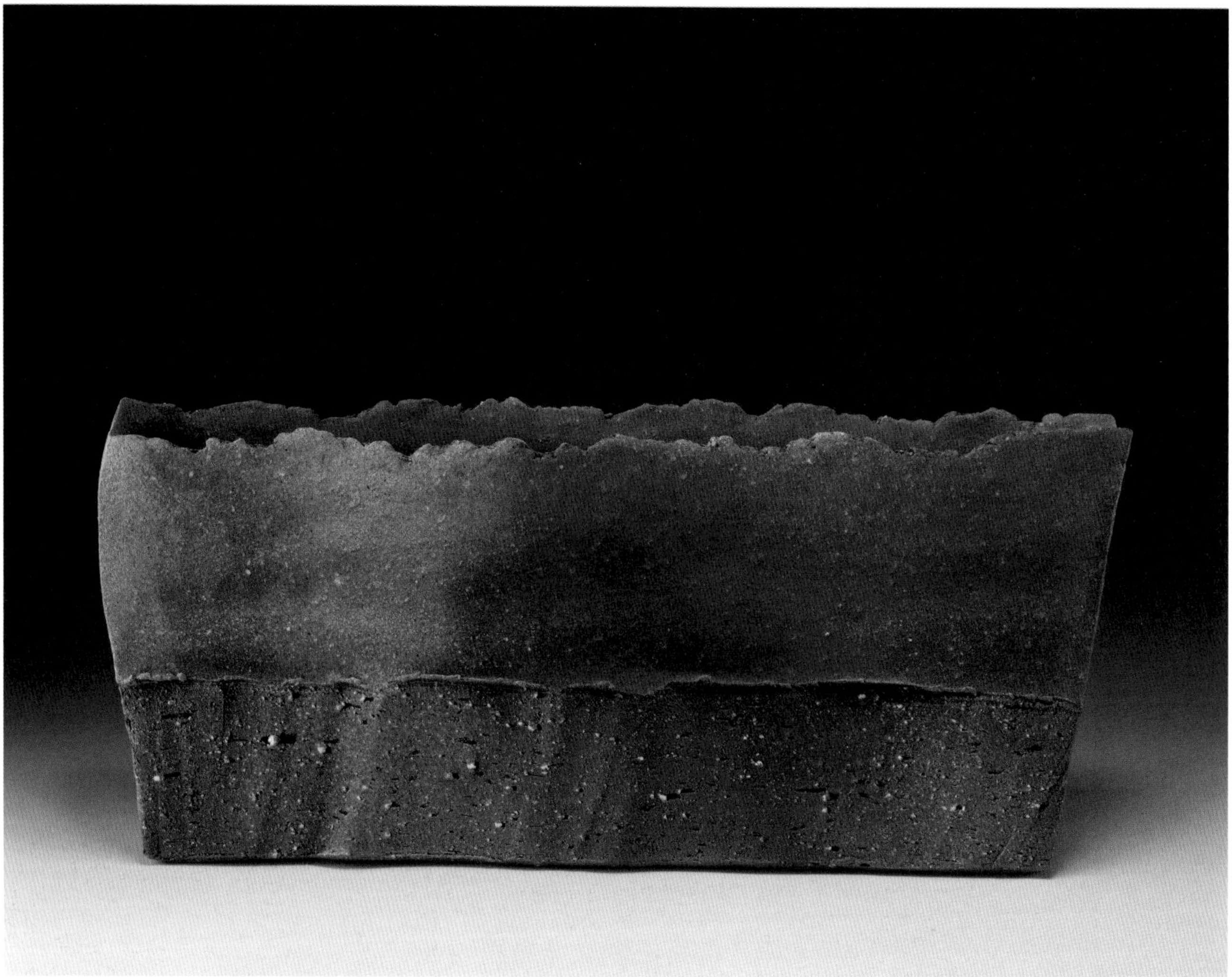

39 Untitled, 2002 ······· 55.5 × 18 × 25.5 cm (21.8 × 7.1 × 10.0 inches) ······· Private Collection
40 Untitled, 2002 ······· 15.4 × 7.2 × 15.6 cm, 24.0 × 10 × 25 cm (6.1 × 2.8 × 6.1 inches, 9.4 × 3.9 × 9.8 inches) ······· Private Collection

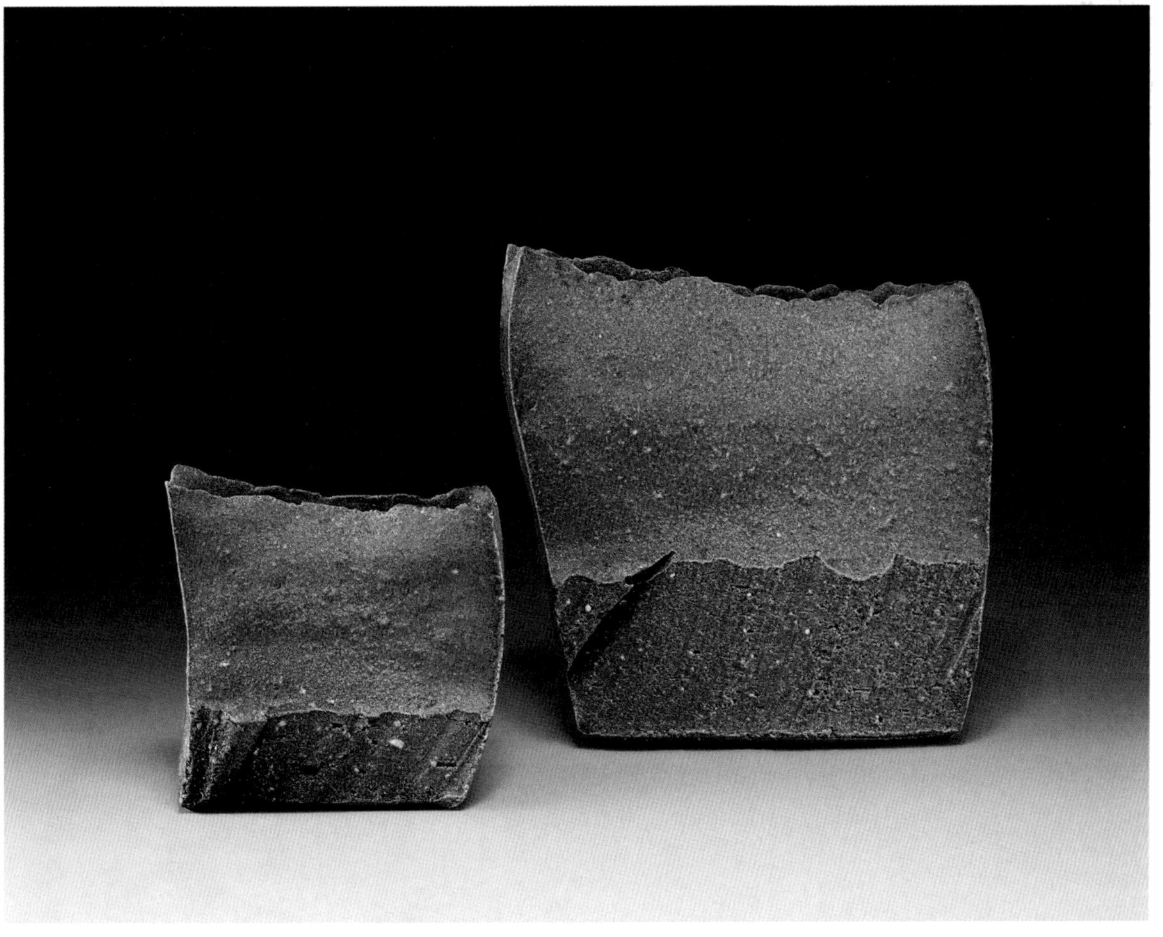

41 Untitled, 2002 ······· 38.0 × 12.5 × 36.2 cm (14.9 × 4.9 × 14.3 inches) ······· Private Collection

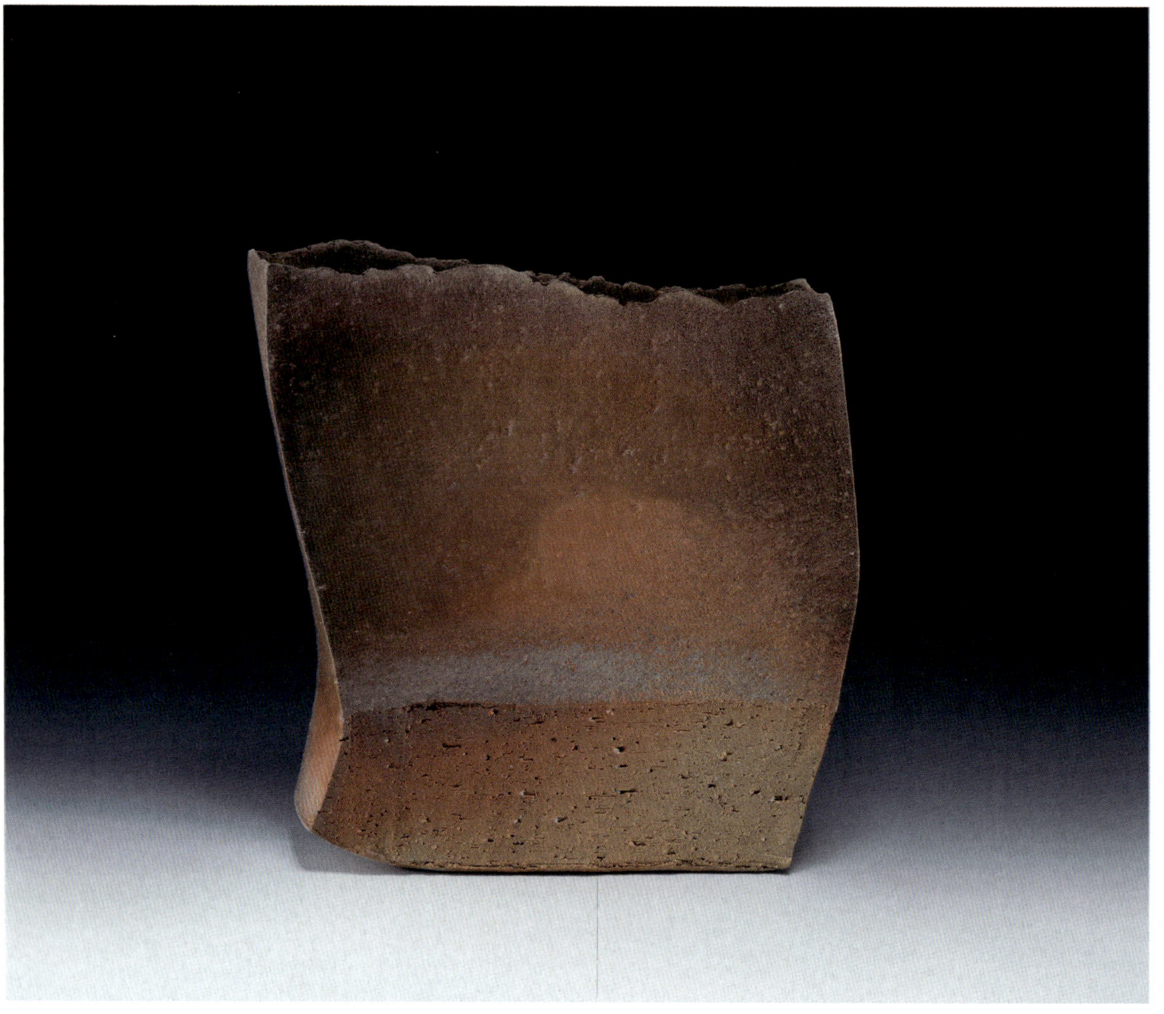

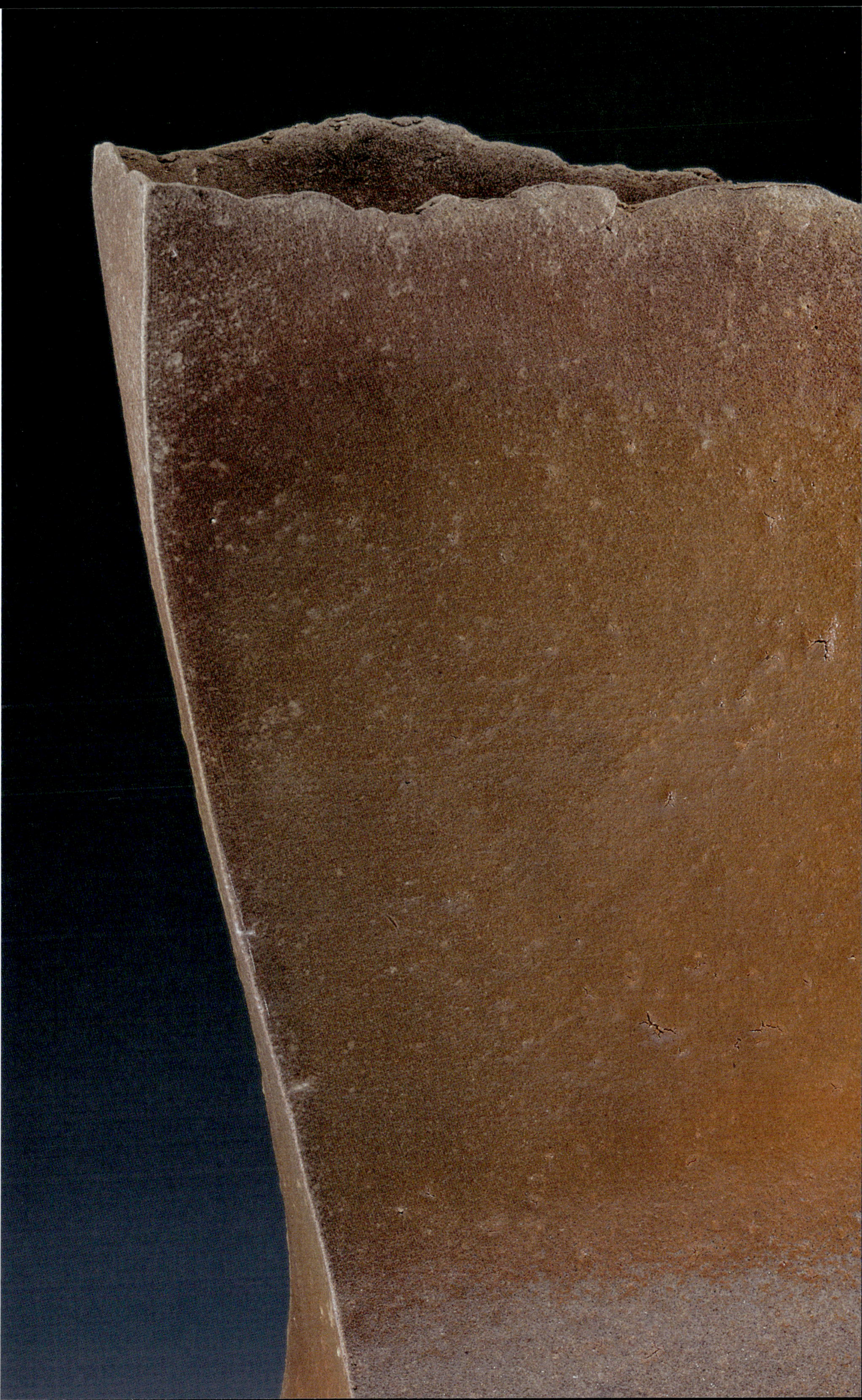

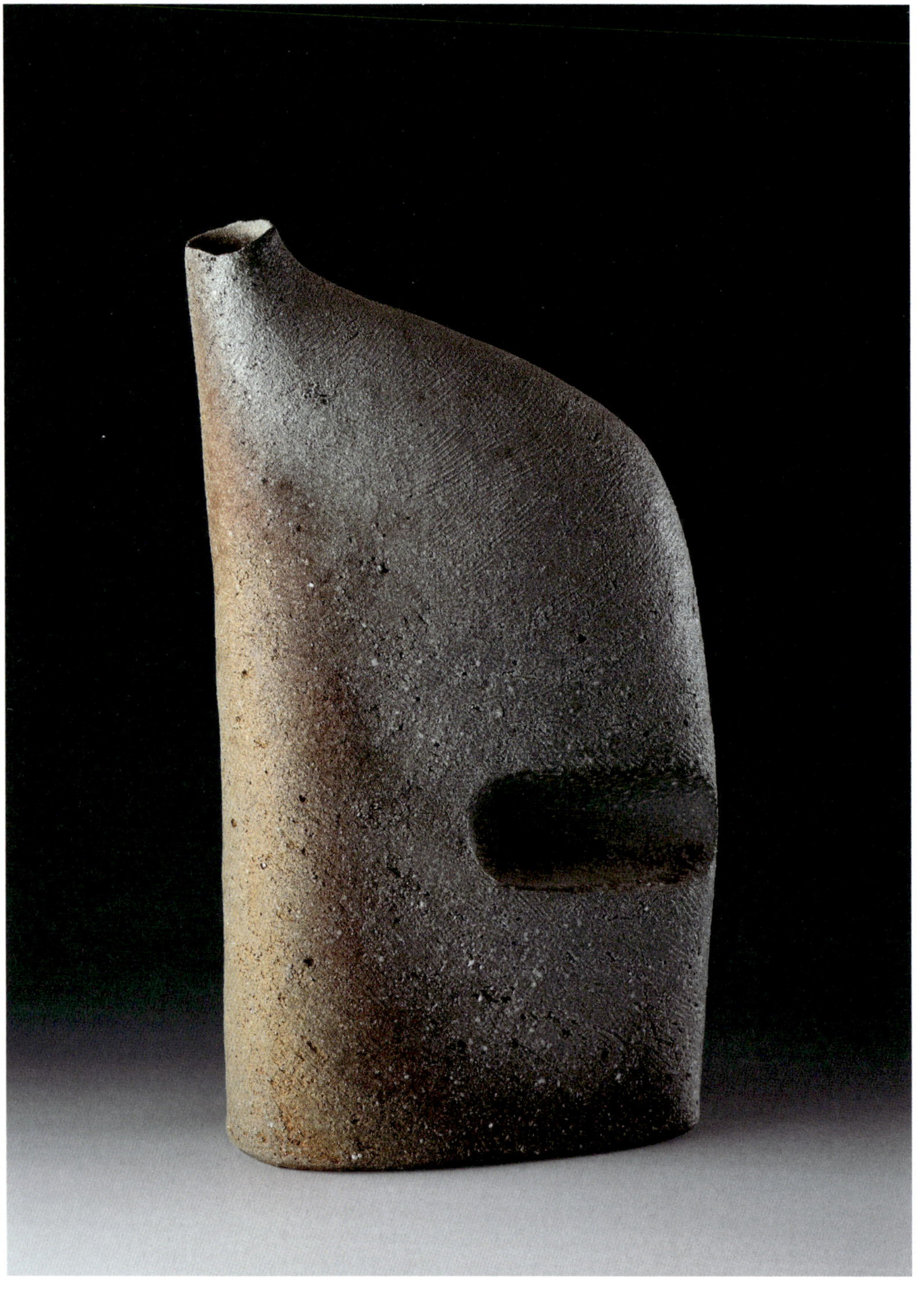

42 Untitled, 2004 ······· 36 × 13 × 55 cm (14.1 × 5.1 × 21.6 inches) ······· Collection of the artist

43 Untitled, 2004 ······· 30 × 15 × 64.5 cm, 30 × 16 × 64.5 cm (11.8 × 5.9 × 25.4 inches, 11.8 × 6.3 × 25.4 inches) ······· Collection of the artist

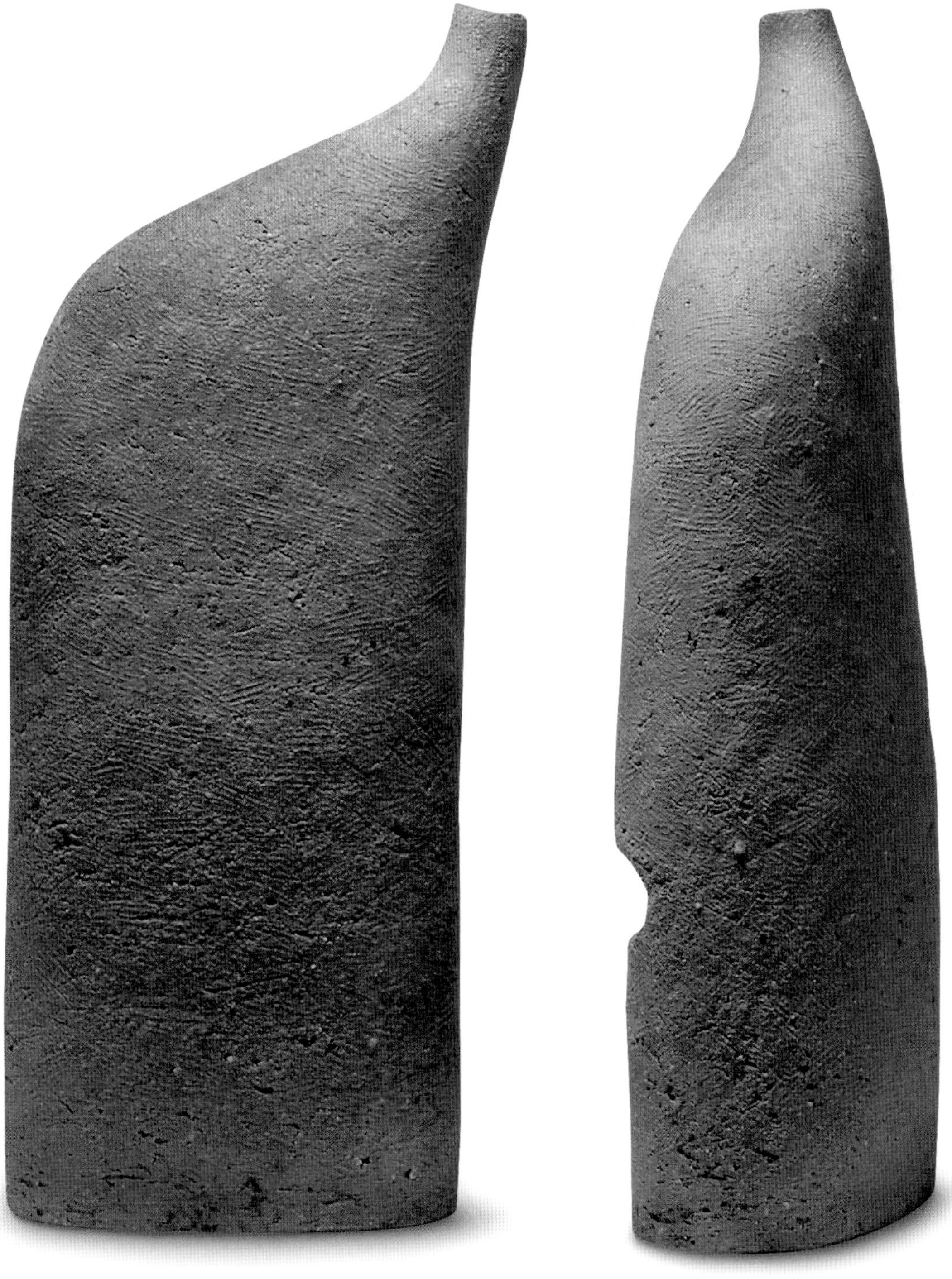

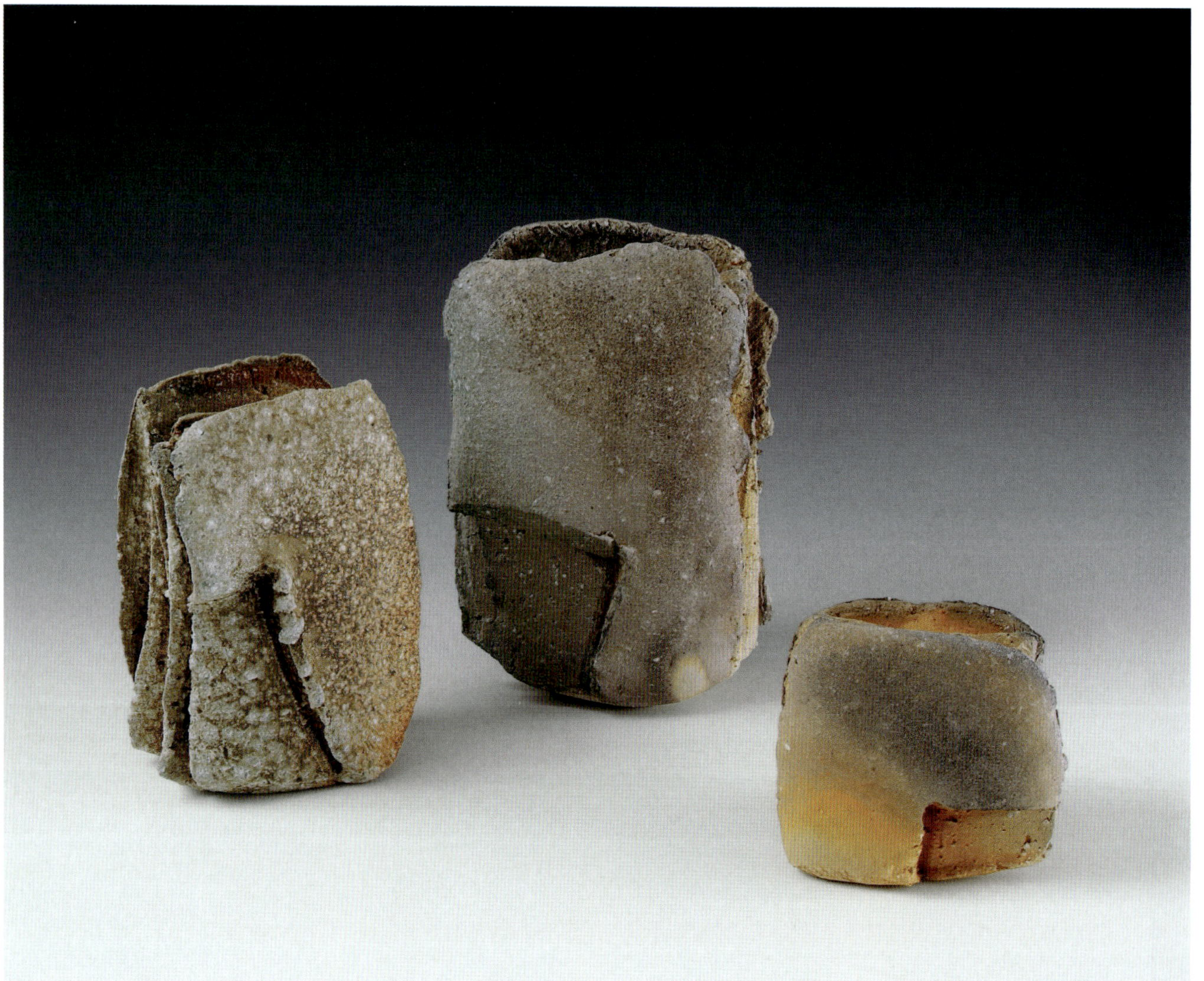

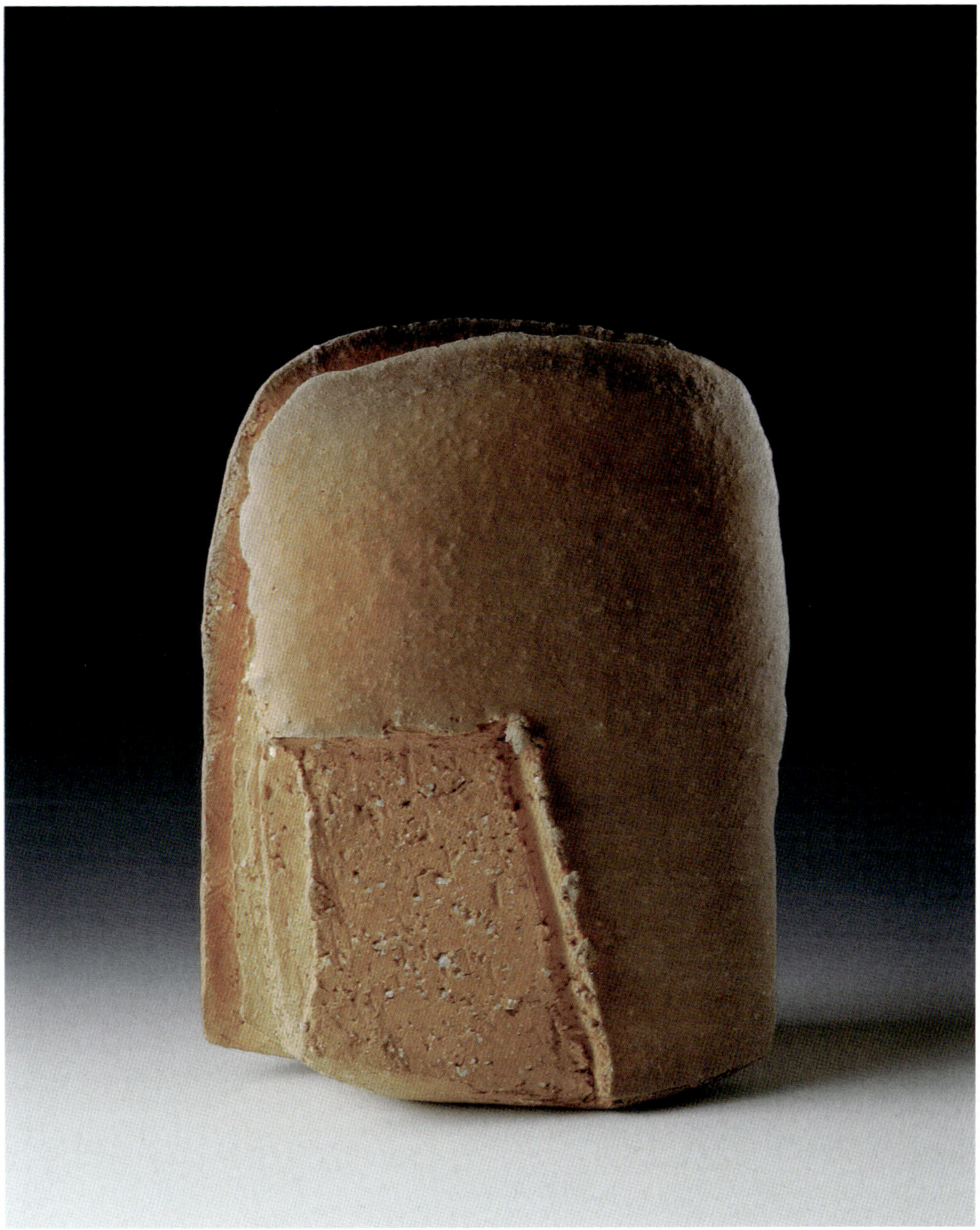

44 TSUCHIKURE, 2007 ······· 10 × 10 × 15.4 cm, 13 × 9.5 × 19.0 cm, 10 × 9 × 9 cm (3.9 × 3.9 × 6.1 inches, 5.1 × 3.7 × 7.5 inches, 3.9 × 3.7 × 3.7 inches) ······· Private Collection

45 TSUCHIKURE, 2008 ······· 20 × 14 × 28 cm (7.9 × 5.5 × 11.0 inches) ······· Collection of the artist

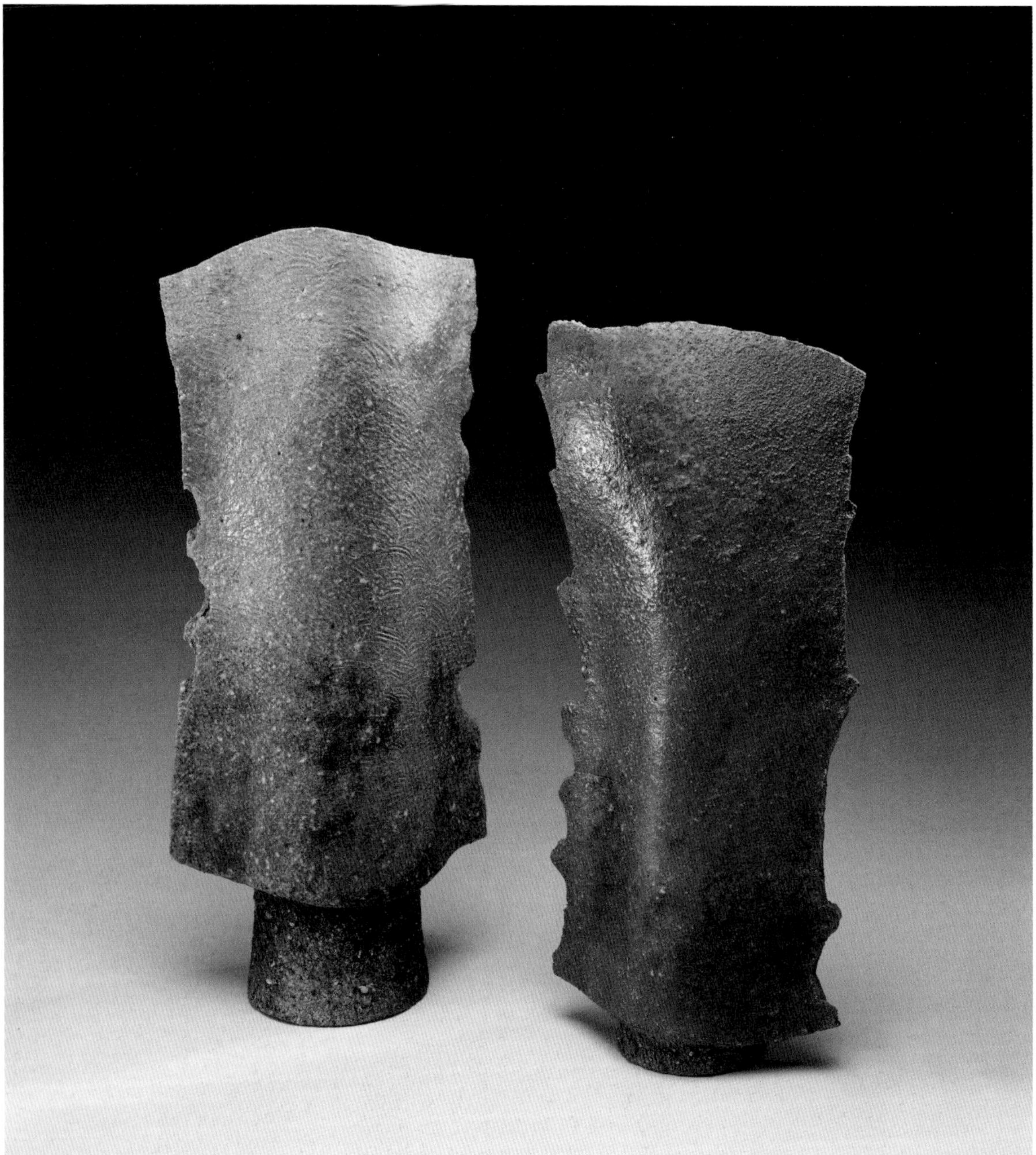

46 Untitled, 1992 ······· 23 × 8 × 47 cm, 22 × 8 × 46 cm (9.0 × 3.1 × 18.5 inches, 8.6 × 3.1 × 18.1 inches) ······· Collection of the artist

47 Untitled, 1992 ······· 28 × 12 × 57 cm (11.0 × 4.7 × 22.4 inches) ······· Collection of the artist

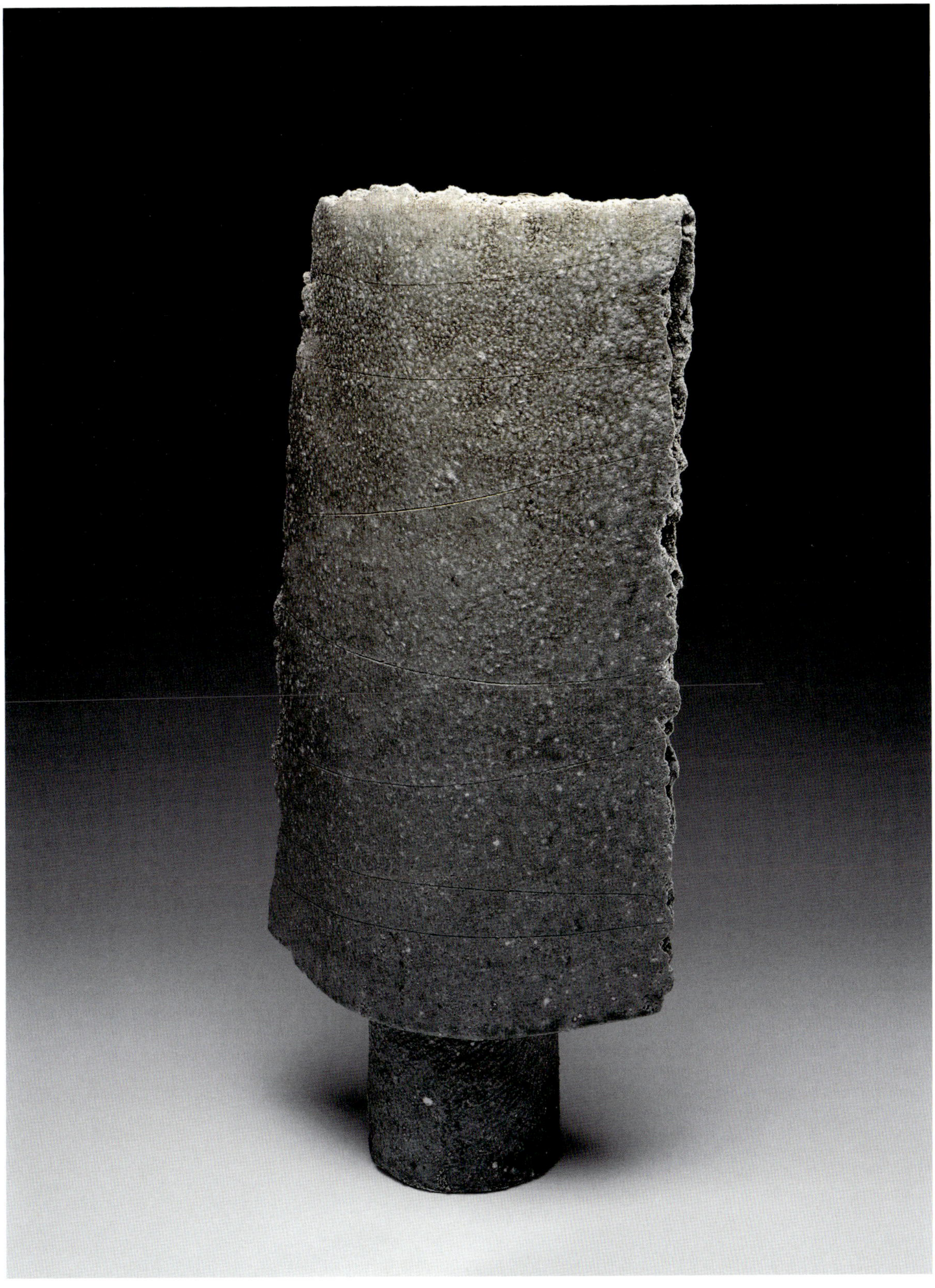

48 DOKI NO NAKAMA, 2008 ······· 32 × 11.5 × 36.5 cm, 42 × 9.5 × 26.0 cm, 21 × 7.5 × 16 cm, 46 × 12.5 × 25 cm, 31 × 8 × 17.5 cm (12.6 × 4.5 × 14.3 inches, 16.5 × 3.7 × 10.2 inches, 8.2 × 2.9 × 6.3 inches, 18.1 × 4.9 × 9.8 inches, 12.2 × 3.1 × 6.8 inches) ······· Collection of the artist

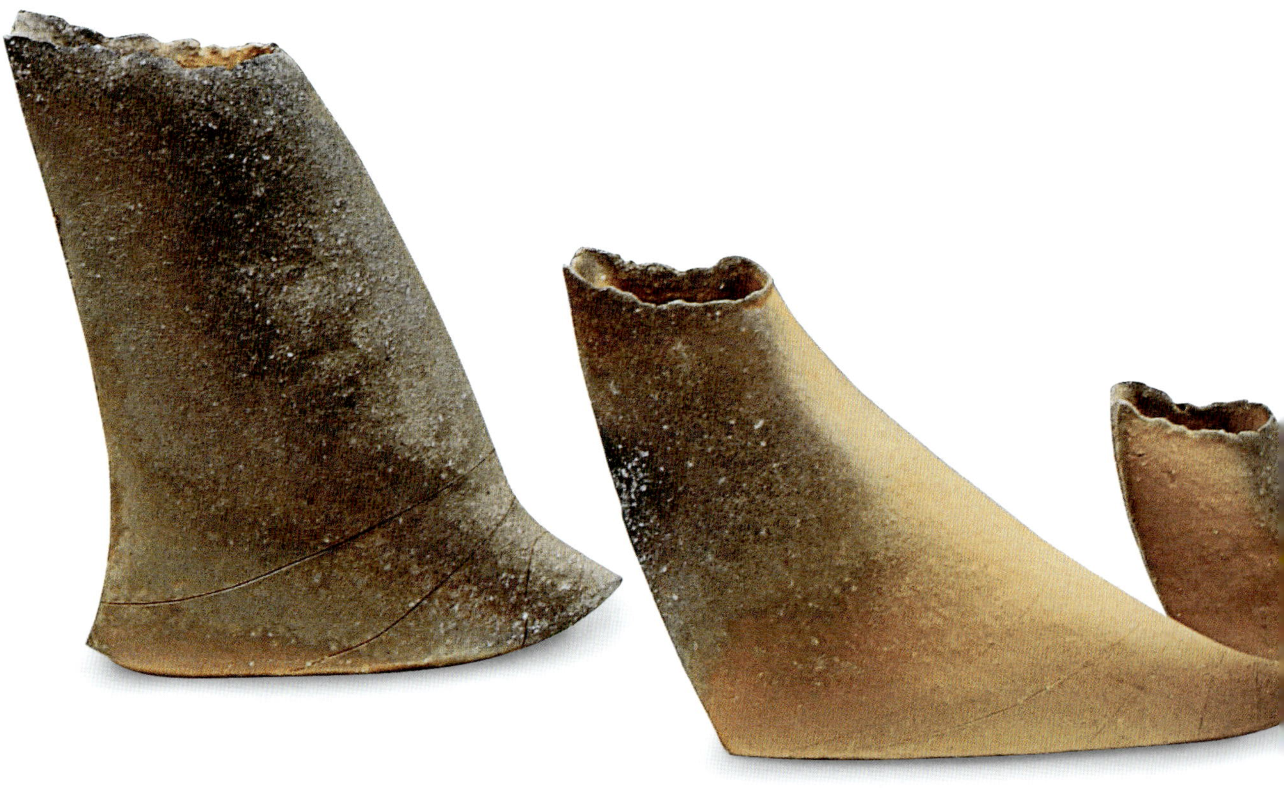

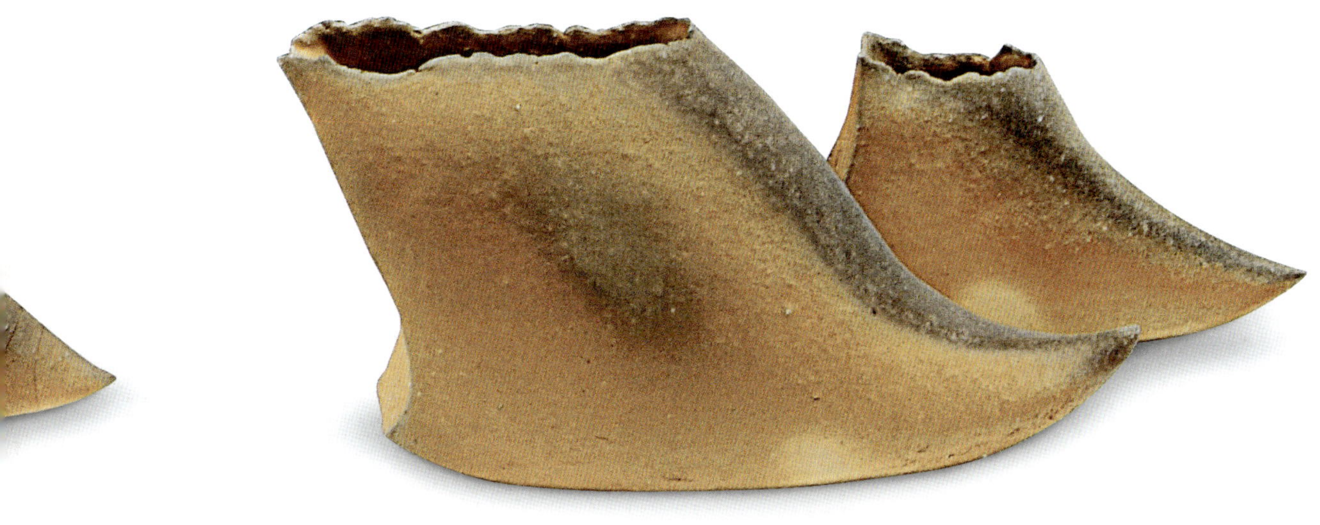

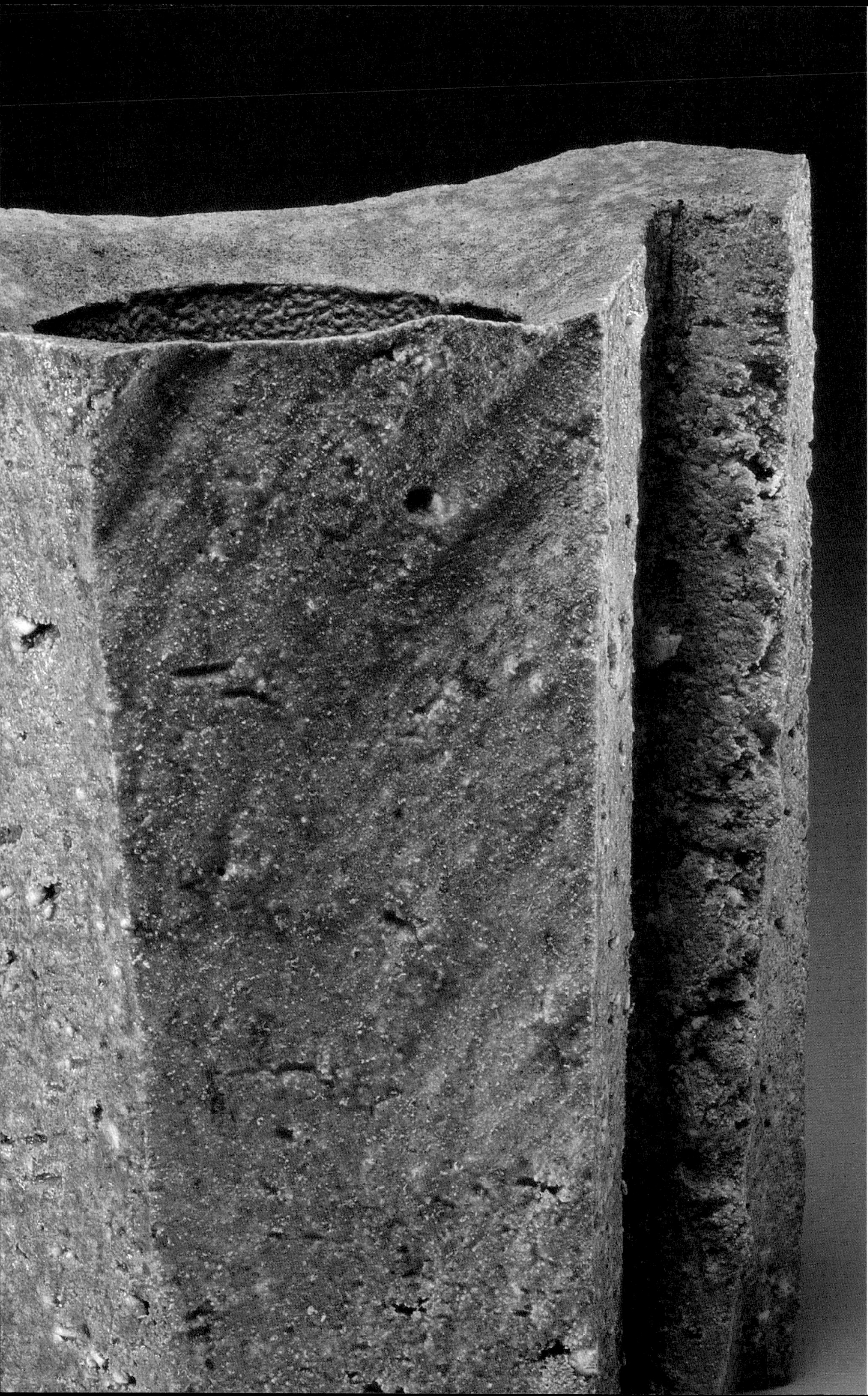

49 Slice of Earth, 1994 ······· 56 × 15 × 30 cm (22.0 × 5.9 × 11.8 inches) ······· Private Collection

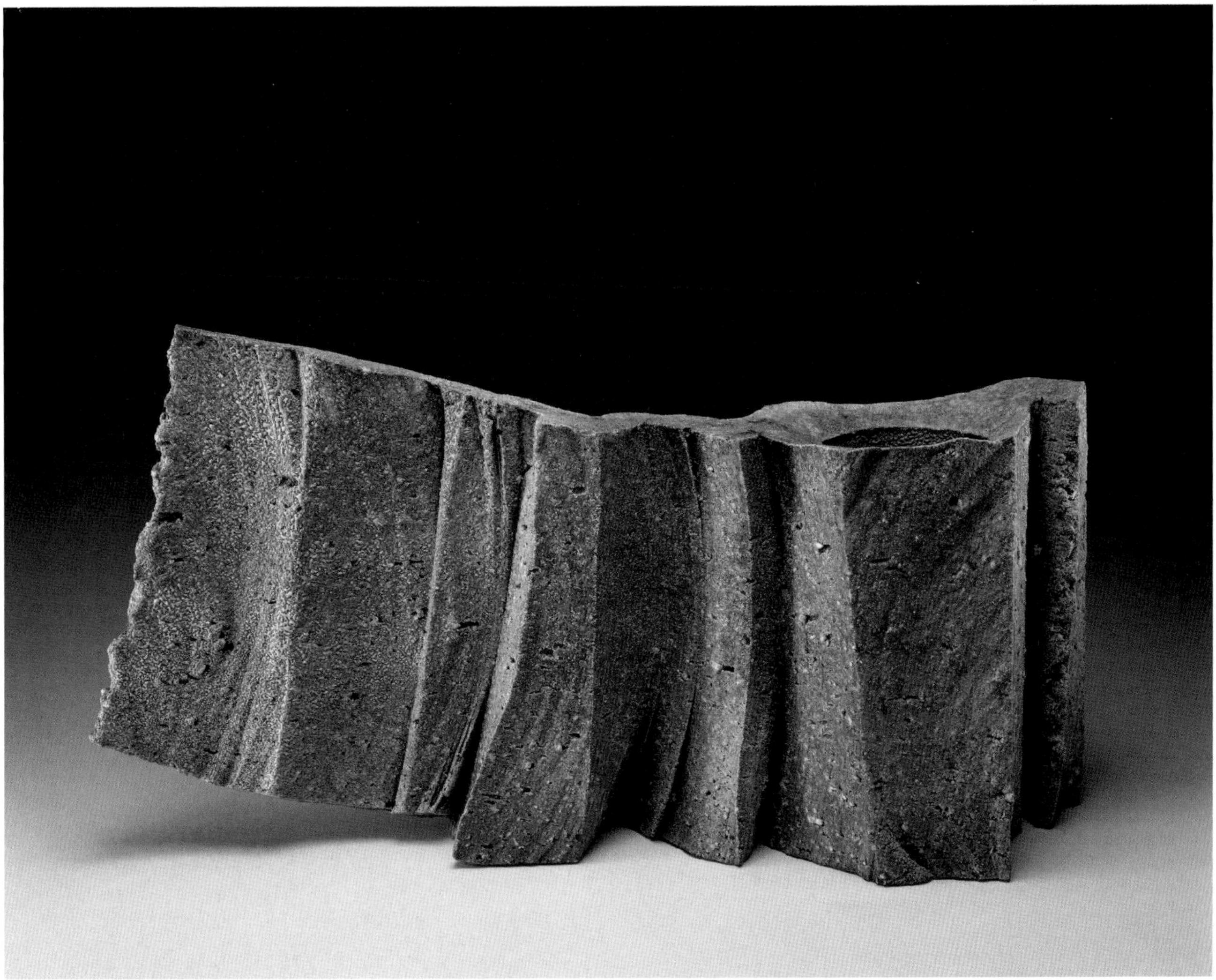

50 DANPEN, 2010 ······· 88 × 24 × 28 cm (34.9 × 9.4 × 14.7 inches) ······· Stanley and Mary Ann Snider Collection, The Museum of Fine Arts, Boston

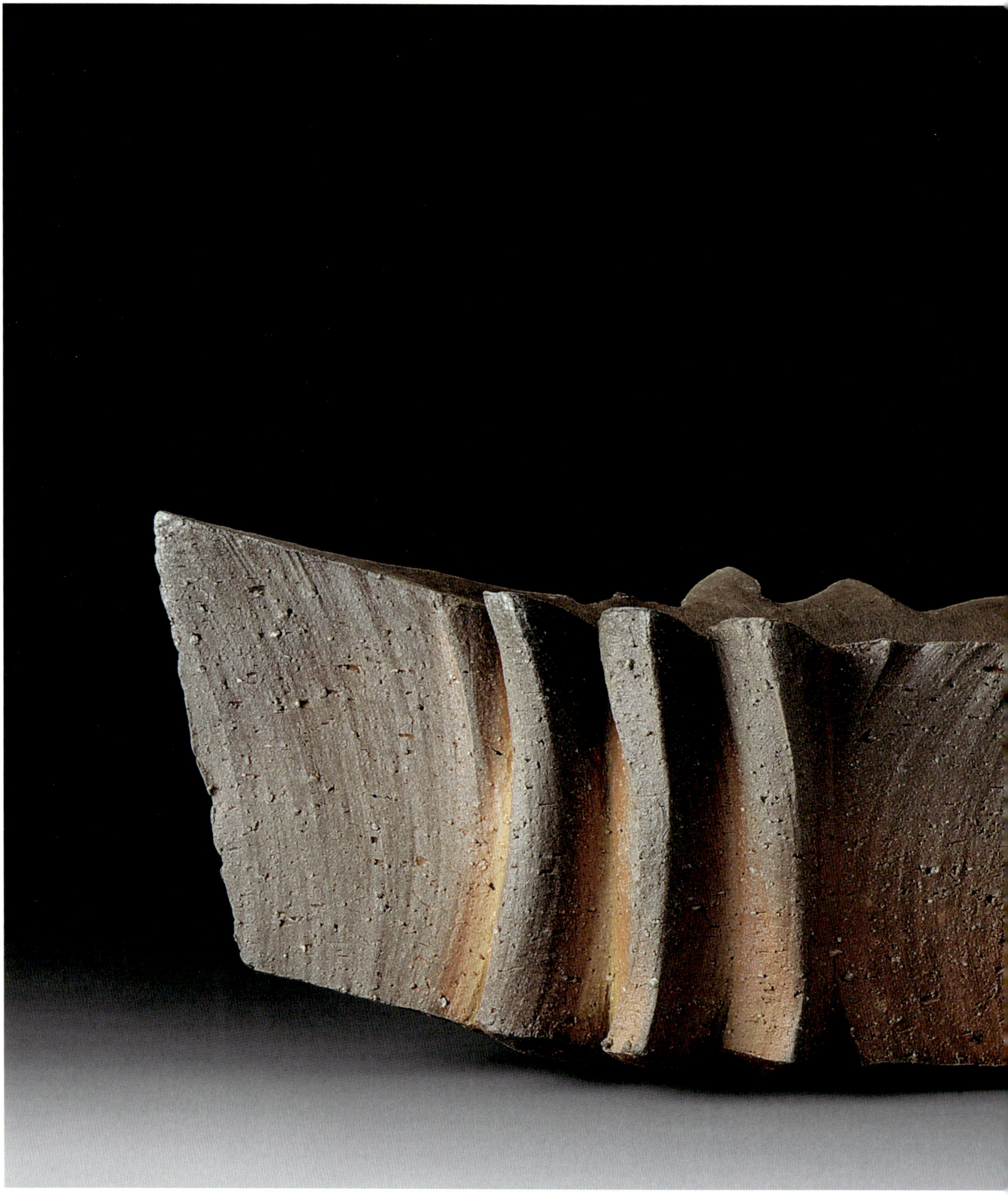

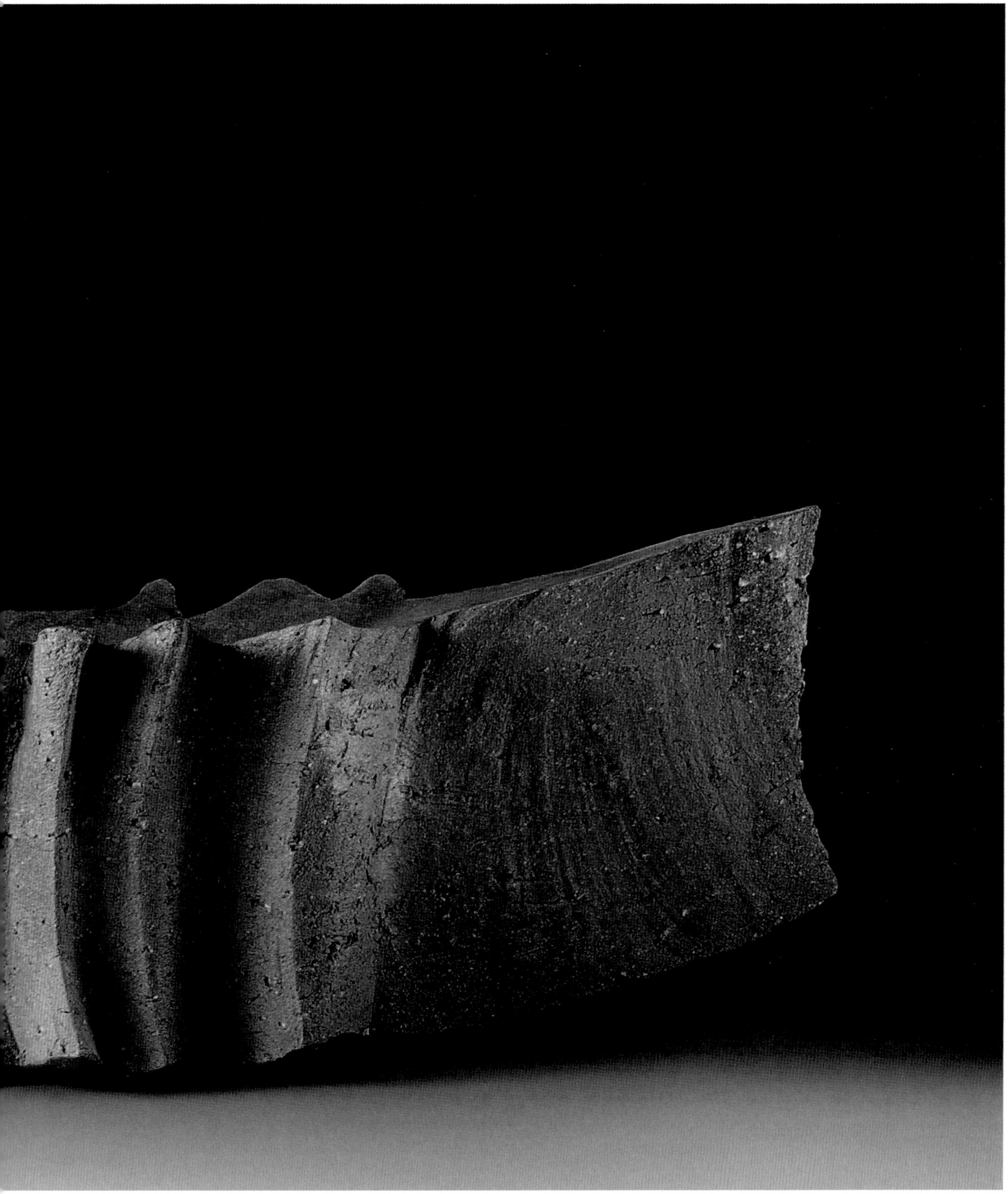

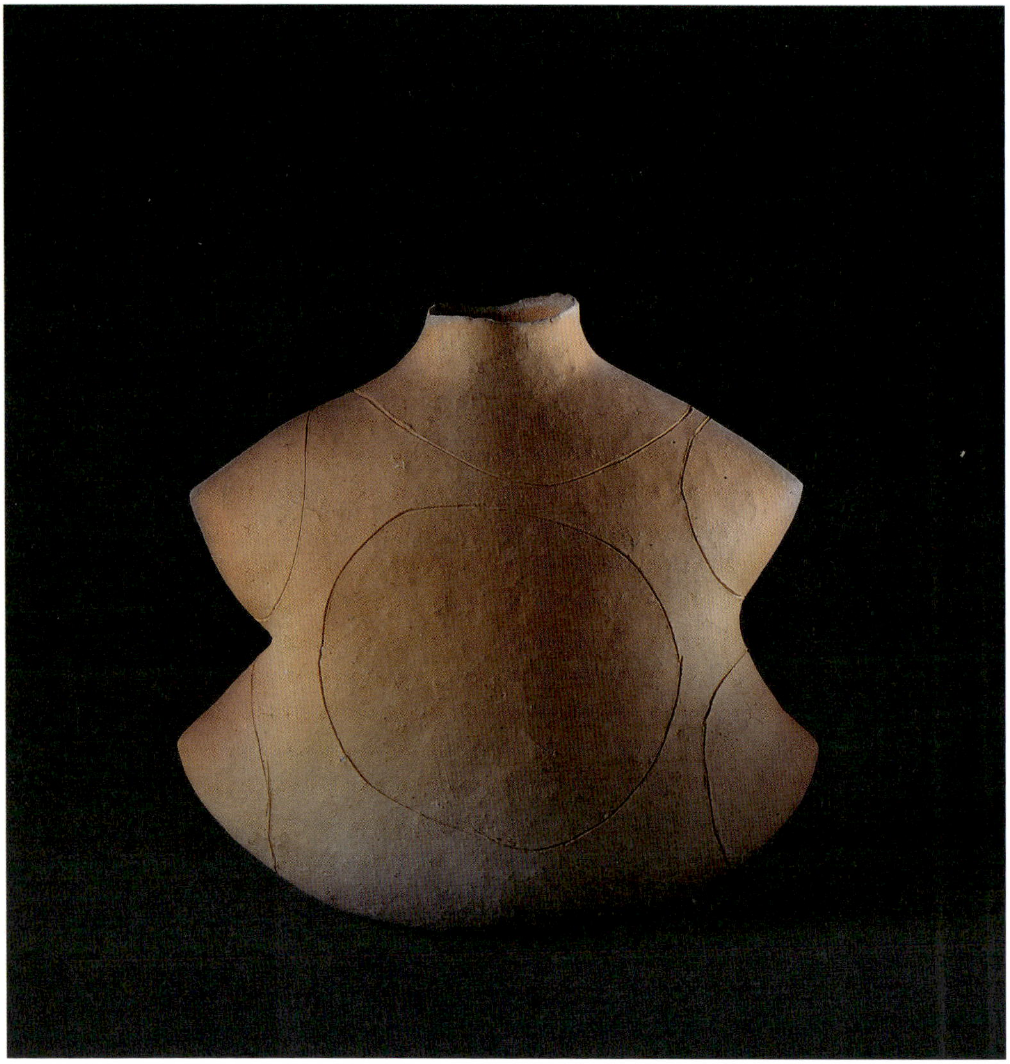

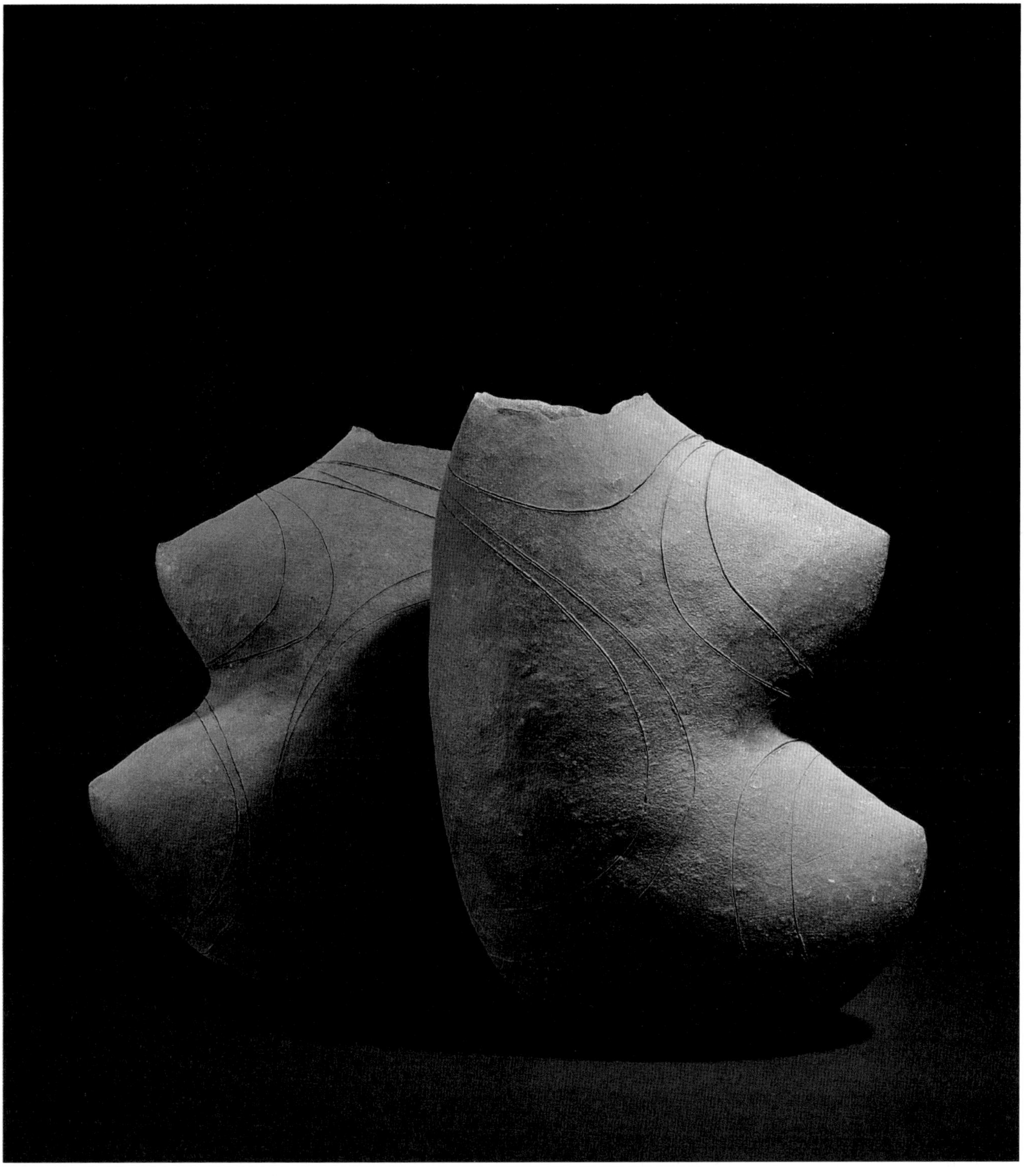

51 SUEMONO, 2010 ······· 23 × 14 × 23 cm (9.0 × 5.5 × 9.0 inches) ······· Private Collection

52 SUEMONO, 2011 ······· 26 × 16 × 31 cm, 23 × 17 × 32 cm (18.1 × 6.3 × 12.2 inches, 9.0 × 6.7 × 12.6 inches) ······· Collection of the artist

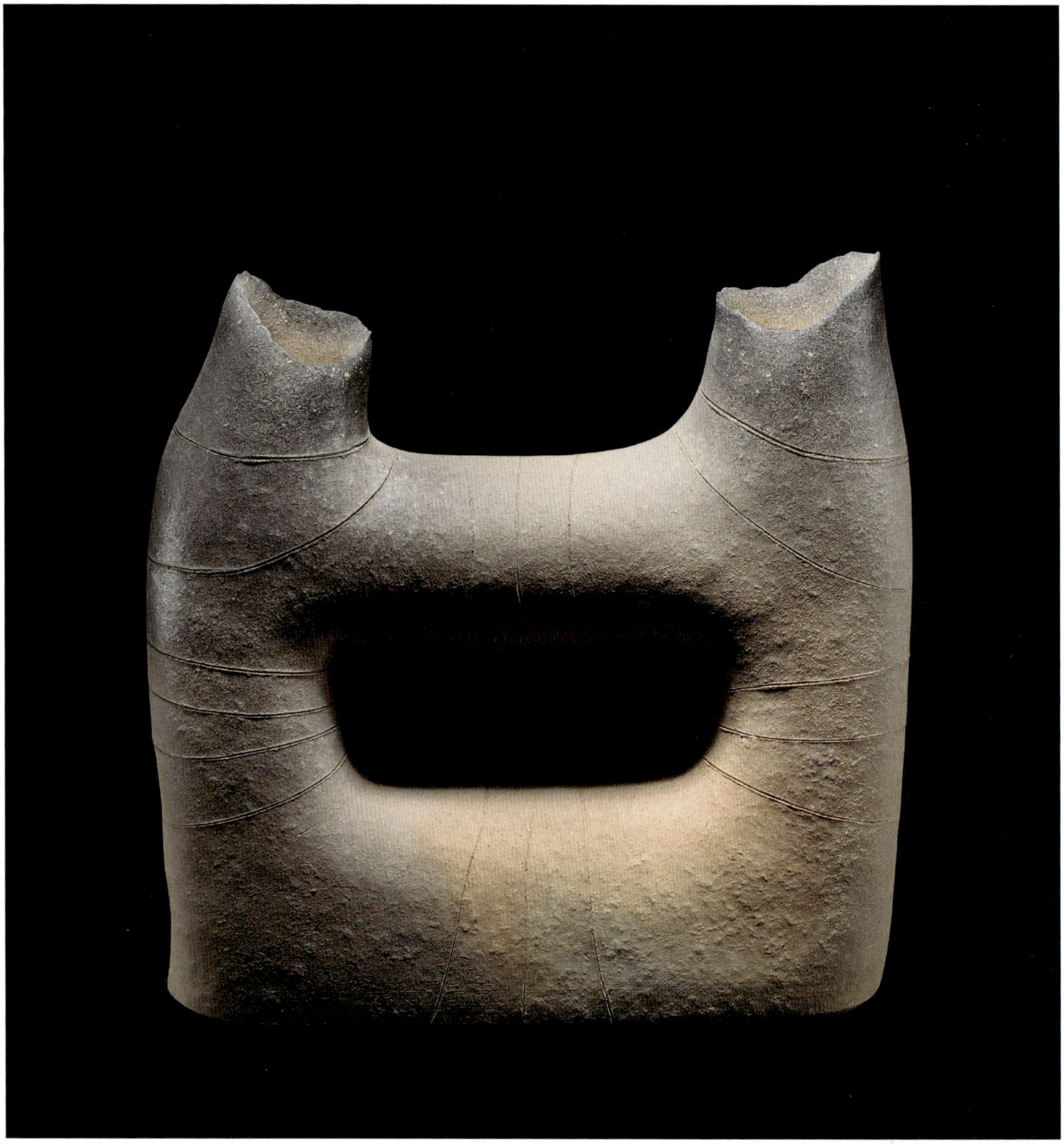

53 SAI, 2008 ······· 32.6 × 10.0 × 32.5 cm (12.8 × 4.0 × 13.0 inches) ······· Samuel and Gabrielle Lurie Collection, New York

54 SUEMONO, 2010 ······· 19 × 10 × 17 cm, 15 × 14 × 24 cm (7.5 × 3.9 × 6.7 inches, 5.9 × 5.5 × 9.4 inches) ······· Private Collection

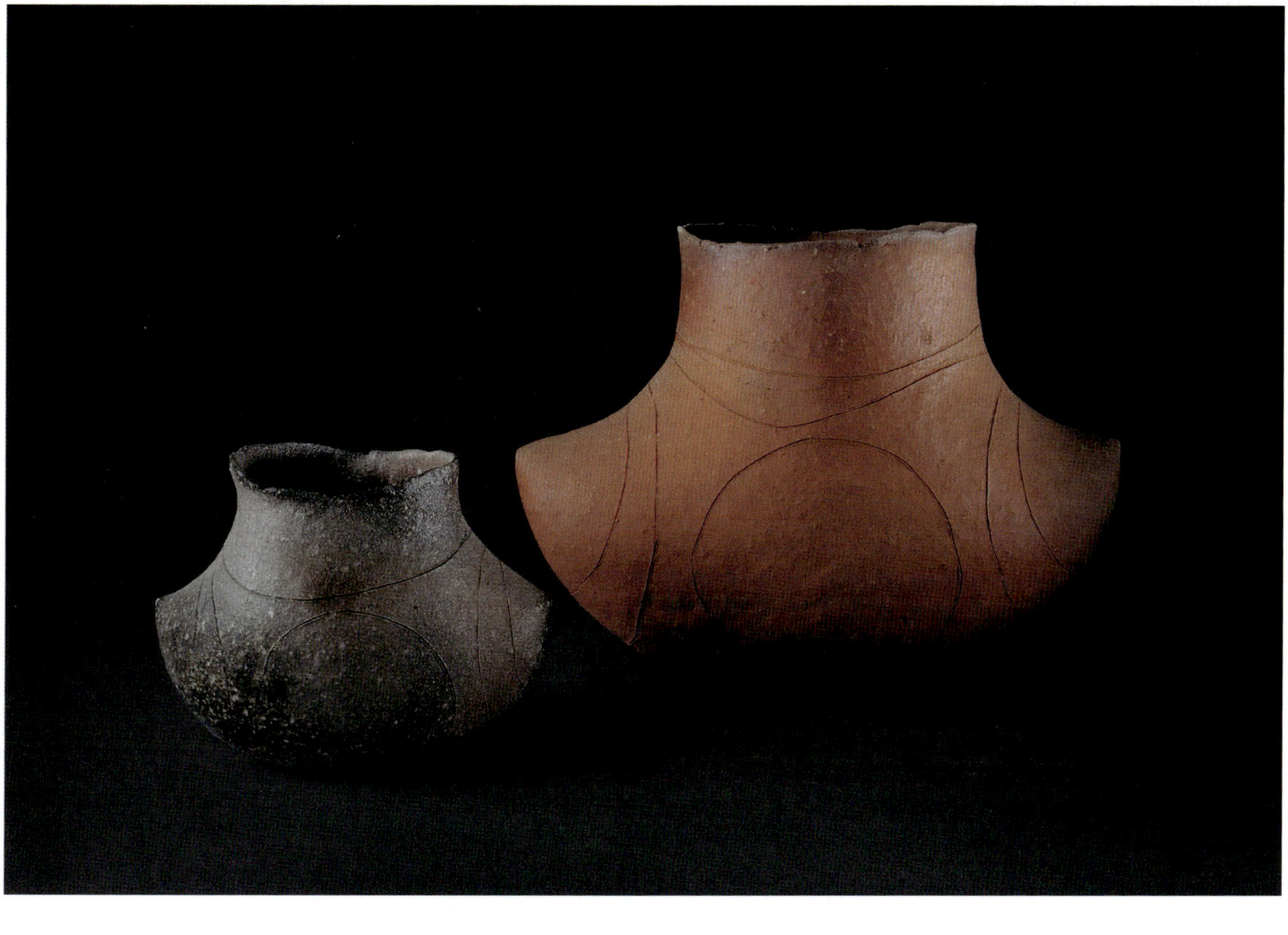

55 Moon, 2010 ······· 17.5 × 14.2 × 31.5 cm (6.9 × 5.6 × 12.4 inches) ······· Stanley and Mary Ann Snider Collection, Museum of Fine Arts, Boston

56 Slice of Earth, 2010 ······· 23 × 14 × 36.5 cm (9.0 × 5.5 × 14.3 inches) ······· LongHouse Reserve

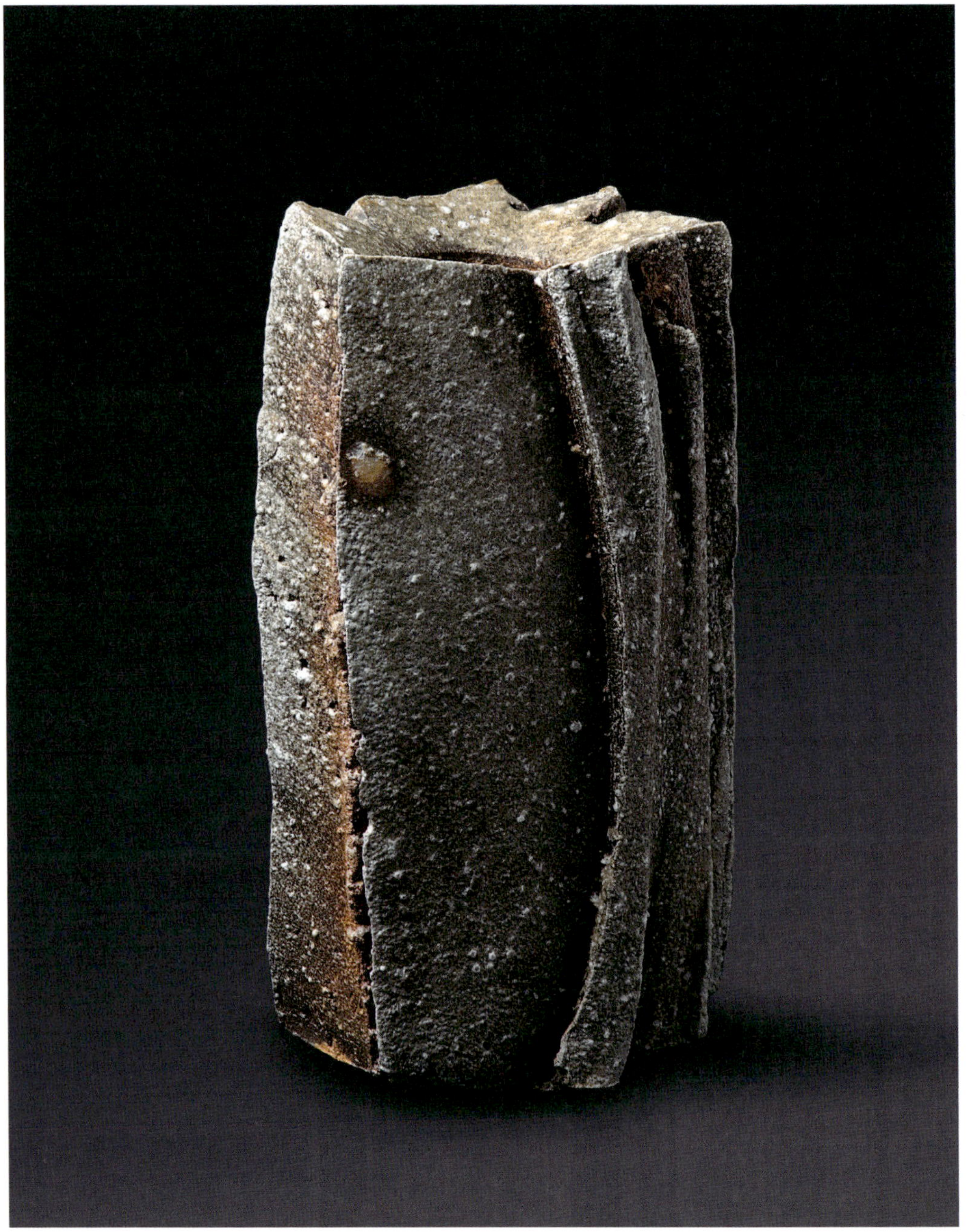

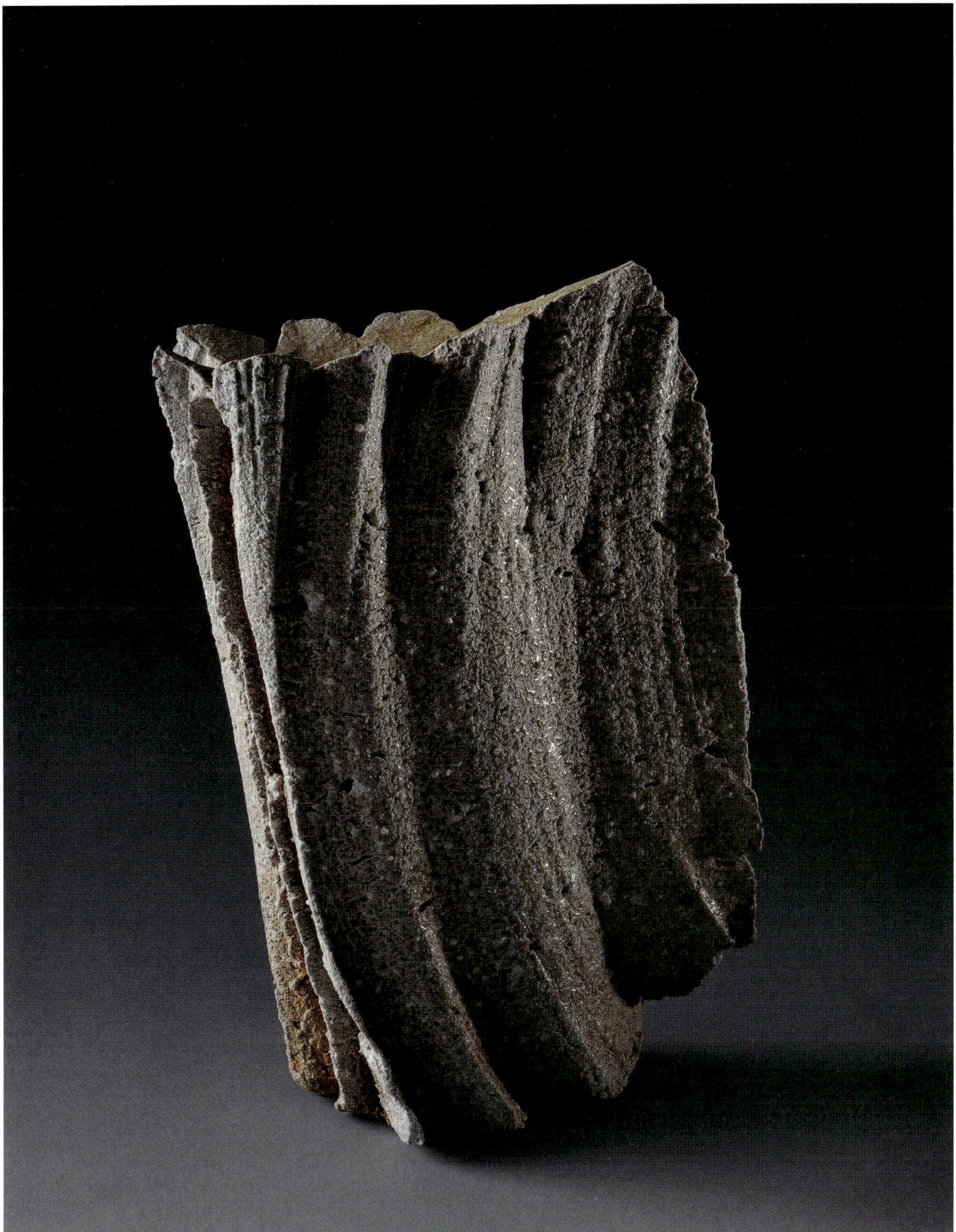

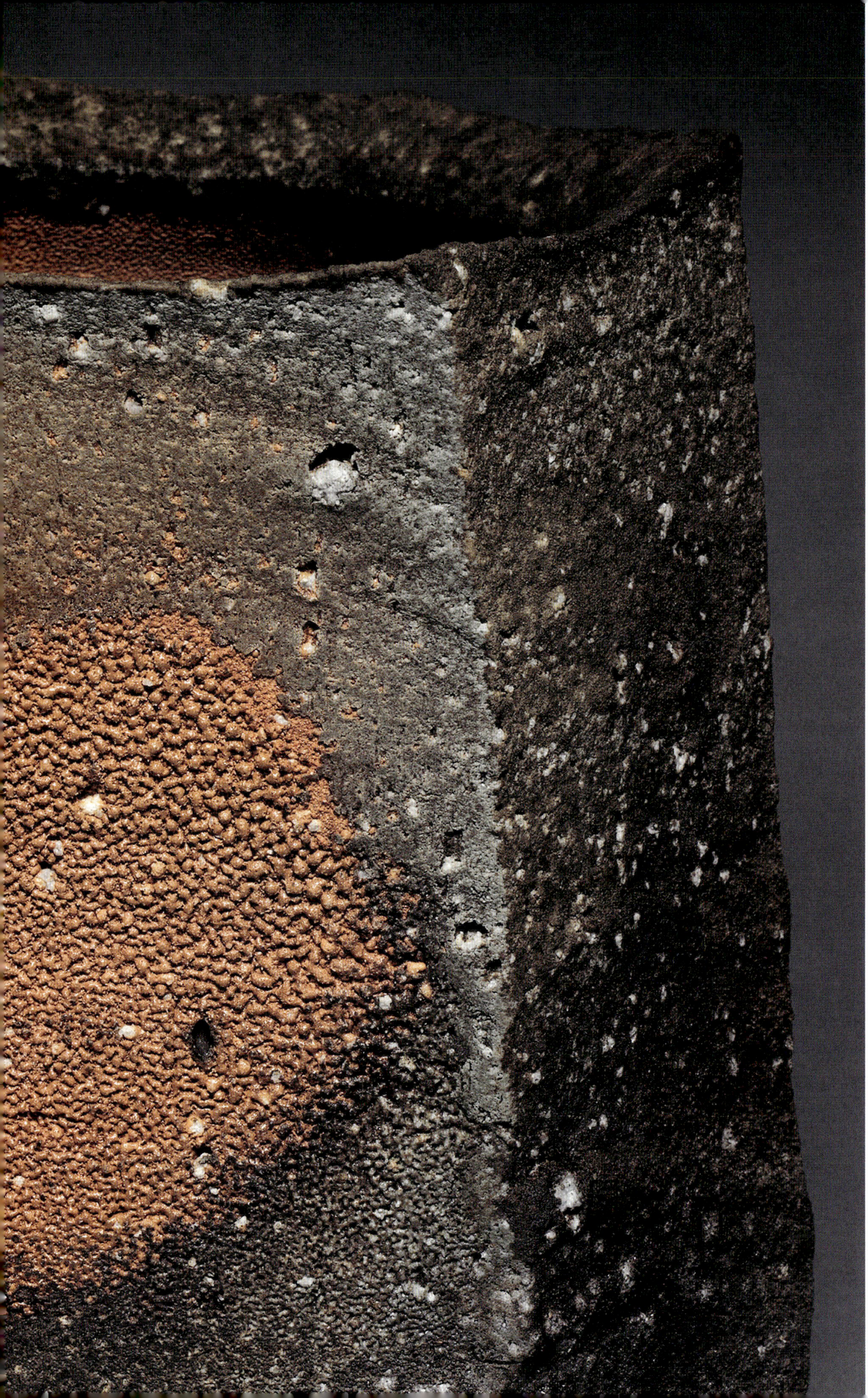

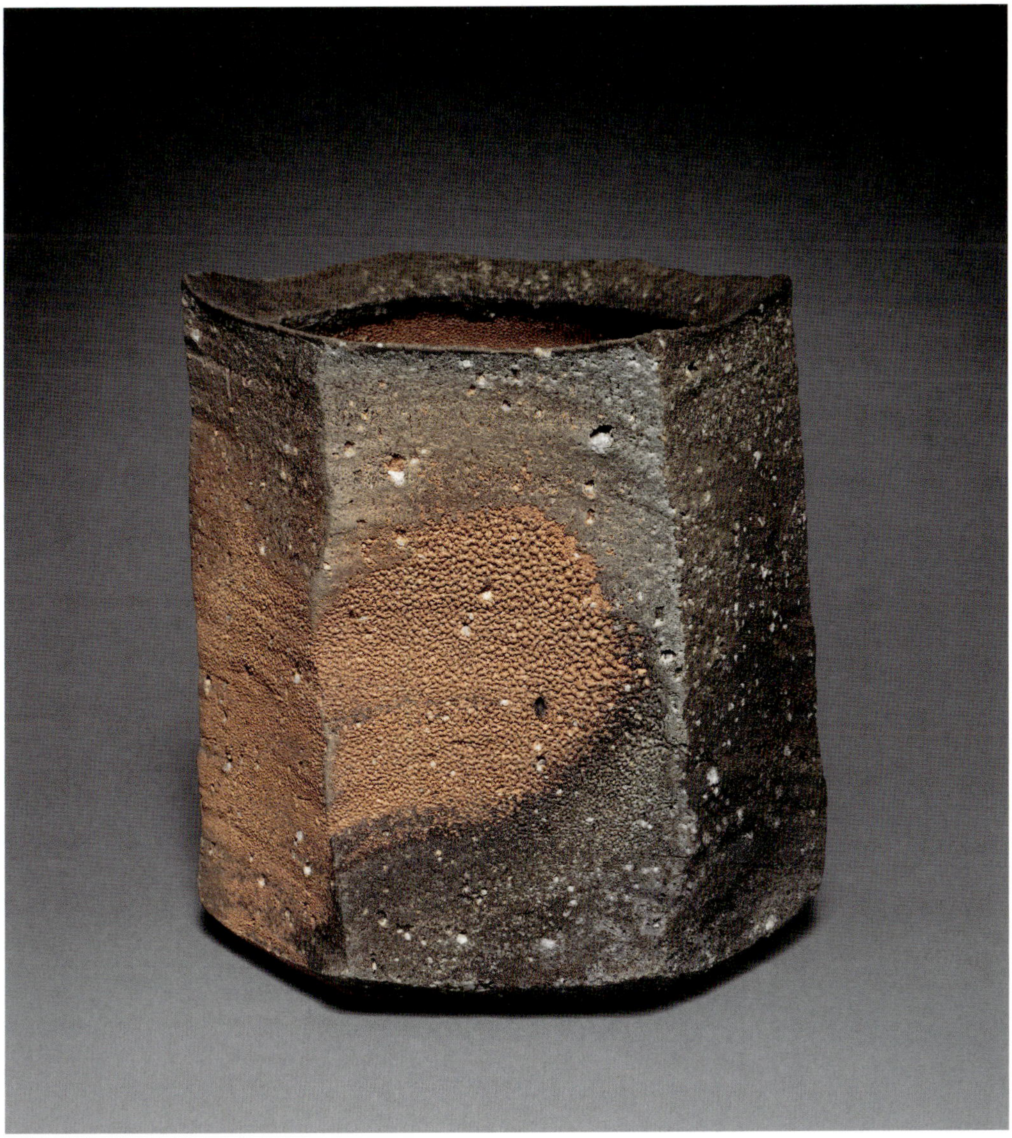

57 Shigaraki Shizenyu MENTORI Vase, 1983 ······· 21.7 × 14.2 × 20.0 cm (8,5 × 5.6 × 7.9 inches) ······· Louis D. Kacalieff, M.D. Fund, The Cleveland Museum of Art, Cleveland

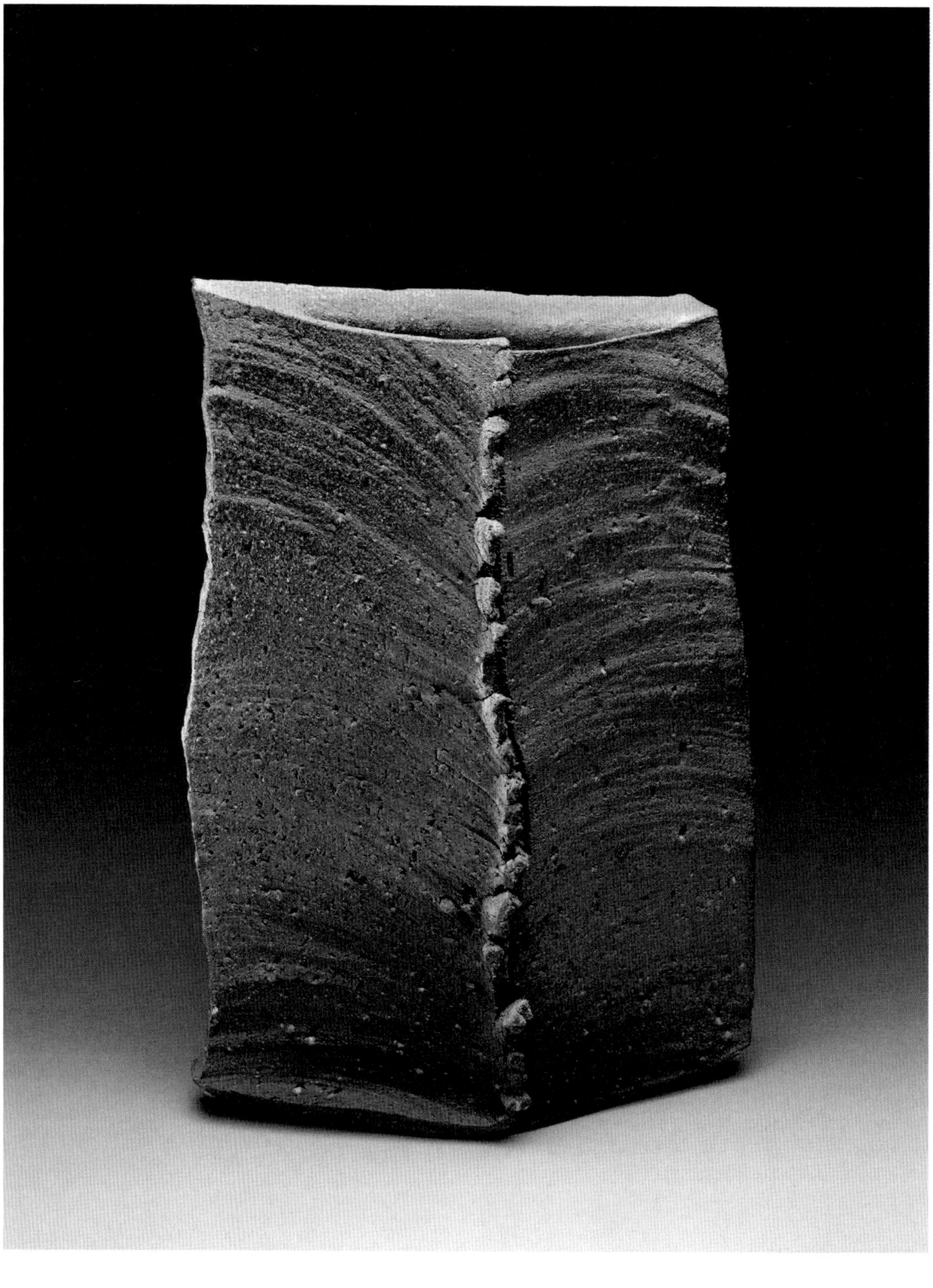

58 Shigaraki Shizenyu MENTORI Vase, 1991 ······· 40 × 14 × 53 cm (10.6 × 5.5 × 20.8 inches) ······· Keramiekmuseum Princessehof, Leeuwarden

Appendix

Biography

Born 1936, Shigaraki, Japan
Lives and works in Shigaraki

2015	Instructor, Ceramics department, National Art School, Sydney NSW, Australia
2014	Instructor, Ceramics program, Office for the Arts at Harvard, Boston MA, USA
2010	Instructor, School of the Museum of Fine Arts, Boston MA, USA
2008	Instructor, The Cleveland Institute of Art, Cleveland OH, and Kent State University, Kent OH, USA
2004	Worked at the Sturt Craft Work Centre, Mittagong NSW, Australia
1999	Instructor, The Cleveland Institute of Art, Cleveland OH, and Kent State University, Kent, OH, USA
1997	Instructor, Huara Huara Studios and lecture at the National Museum of Santiago de Chile, Chile
1996	Worked at Atelier du CEP, Aube, France
1993	Instructor, The Cleveland Institute of Art, Cleveland OH, and Kent State University, Kent OH, USA
1992	Worked at the European Ceramic Work Center, 's-Hertogenbosch, The Netherlands
1969	Revived use of the traditional Japanese *anagama* natural firing kiln in order to reproduce classical style pottery
1955	Studied with ceramic designer Sakuzo Hineno

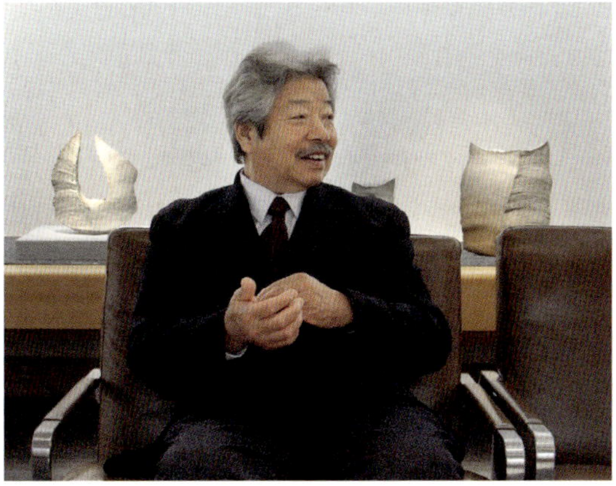

Awards

2010	SOFA New York, LongHouse Reserve Special Recognition Award for Best Artwork in Show
1983	Shinkougei Exhibition Award
1982	The Japan Fine Arts Exhibition Award
	Shinkougei Exhibition Award
1970	Japanese Craft for Flower Arrangement and Tea Ceremony Award
	Dentoukougei Exhibition Award
1964	Asahi Ceramic Art Exhibition Award
	Contemporary Crafts Exhibition Award
	Japanese Ceramic Design for Export Exhibition Award
1959	Shiga Art Exhibition Award

2001 *Great Shigaraki*, The Museum of Contemporary Ceramic Arts, The Shigaraki Ceramic Cultural Park, Shiga, Japan

2000 SOFA-NY, browngrotta arts, USA
400 years anniversary: Japan and the Netherlands, Galerie De Witte Voet, Amsterdam, The Netherlands
Ceramics, Lew Allen Contemporary, Santa Fe NM, USA

1999 SOFA-NY, browngrotta gallery, USA

1998 SOFA-NY, Chicago, browngrotta gallery, USA
Contemporary Ceramics: Selections from the Metropolitan Museum of Art, The Metropolitan Museum of Art, New York City, USA

1994 Kohyama Studio Crafts, Toraya Gallery, New York City, USA

1993 *Application Art Collection by Benno Premsela*, Stedelijk Museum, Amsterdam, The Netherlands
Contemporary Japanese Ceramics, Mitsukoshi Art Gallery, Osaka, Japan
Japanese Crafts Exhibition, Tokyo, Japan (also in 1992, 1959)

1992 Kohyama Studio Crafts, Washikurabu, Osaka, Japan
Kohyama Studio Crafts, Kokyouan Gallery, Osaka, Japan
Kohyama Studio Crafts, Matsuzakaya Art Gallery, Yokkaichi, Japan
Continuity and Transformation: Contemporary Japanese Ceramics. Collection of the Everson Museum of Art, Everson Museum of Art, Syracuse NY, USA

1991 Kohyama Studio Crafts, Daimaru Art Gallery, Osaka, Japan
Kohyama Studio Crafts, Toubien, Nara, Japan
Contemporary Japanese Ceramics, Mitsukoshi Art Gallery, Osaka, Japan

1990 Kohyama Studio Crafts, Toyota Avenue Gallery, Nara, Japan
Primitivism in Contemporary Ceramics, The Museum of Contemporary Ceramic Arts, The Shigaraki Ceramic Cultural Park, Shiga, Japan

1989 Kohyama Studio Crafts, Ginza Matsuya, Tokyo, Japan
Kohyama Studio Crafts, Uchida Hall, Osaka, Japan
Kohyama Studio Crafts, Gallery Kaita, Tokyo, Japan (also in 1988, 1987, 1986, 1985)

1988 Kohyama Studio Crafts, Hosaka Gallery, Yamanashi, Japan
Kohyama Studio Crafts, Higashioji Gallery, Nara, Japan

1986 Kohyama Studio Crafts, Takashimaya, Kyoto, Japan
Ikebana International, Takashimaya Art Gallery, Kyoto, Japan

1985 Kohyama Studio Crafts, Daimaru, Osaka, Japan

1984 Kohyama Studio Crafts, Gakuenmae Art Gallery, Nara, Japan

1983 *Shinkougei Exhibition*, Kyoto, Japan (also in 1982)

1982 *The Japan Fine Arts Exhibition*, Kyoto, Japan

1979 *Japanese Arts and Crafts Show*, private house, Los Angeles, USA
Kohyama Studio Crafts, Ginza Matsuya, Tokyo, Japan

1978 *Contemporary Ceramics by Five Artists*, Tousenbou, Kyoto, Japan

1970 *Japanese Craft for Flower Arrangement and Tea Ceremony*, Kyoto, Japan
Dentoukougei Exhibition, Kyoto, Japan

1967 *Shigaraki Four Artists Exhibition*, Matsuya Ginza, Tokyo, Japan
Shigaraki Crafts Exhibition, Beni Gallery, Kyoto, Japan
Shigaraki New Work Exhibition, Sogo, Kobe, Japan

1966 *Components of Modern Interior Exhibition*, Kyoto Interior Consultant, Kyoto and Nikku, Fukuoka, Japan
Young Artists in Shigaraki Exhibition, Maruzen, Tokyo, Japan

1964 *Asahi Ceramic Art Exhibition*, Nagoya, Japan,
Contemporary Crafts Exhibition, Maruei, Nagoya, Japan
Japanese Ceramic Design for Export Exhibition, Kyoto, Japan

1959 *Shiga Art Exhibition*, Shiga, Japan

1958 *Shigaraki Seitoukai Crafts Exhibition*, Shigakaikan, Shiga, Japan

1957 *Shigaraki Seitoukai Crafts Exhibition*, Shigaraki Kankou Kaikan, Shiga, Japan

Bibliography

Adlin, Jane, 1998. *Contemporary Ceramics: Selections from the Metropolitan Museum of Art*, New York: The Metropolitan Museum of Art.

Albano, Ann, 2009. "The Cleveland Ceramics of Yasuhisa Kohyama", Cleveland: The Sculpture Center.

Bradford, Kelvin, 2010. "Yasuhisa Kohyama Shigaraki Icon", in *Ceramics Monthly,* June–August.

Clayton, Jacqueline, 2005. "Yasuhisa Kohyama Mittagong no Kaze", Sydney: The Ceramic Art Gallery.

Clifford, Shirley, 2004. "Yasuhisa Kohyama Modern Shigaraki Potter", in *Ceramics Art and Perception* 55.

Cunningham, Michael R., 1994. "Slice of Earth: Yasuhisa Kohyama", New York: Toraya Gallery.

Cunningham, Michael R., 1995. "Yasuhisa Kohyama in Exhibitions", in *American Ceramics* 11/4.

Cunningham, Michael R., 1997. "Yasuhisa Kohyama: Impression in Form", Kyoto: Takashimaya Art Gallery.

Earle, Joe, 2005. *Contemporary Clay: Japanese Ceramics for the New Century,* Boston: The Museum of Fine Arts.

Fischer, Felice, 2003. "Yasuhisa Kohyama", Kyoto: Takashimaya Art Gallery.

Grotta, Tom and Brown, Rhonda, 2001. *Stimulus: Art and its Inception,* Wilton: browngrotta gallery.

Honda, Shizuo, 1973. "Dentou wo Ikasuhito", Nagoya: Maruei Art Gallery.

Inui, Yoshiaki, 1990. *"Primitivism" in Contemporary Ceramics,* Shiga: The Museum of Contemporary Ceramic Arts, The Shigaraki Ceramic Cultural Park.

Jefferies, Susan, 1992. "Yasuhisa Kohyama", Tokyo: Takashimaya Gallery.

Kohyama, Yasuhisa, 2015: "Inspirations of Time and Place", in *The Log Book,* issue 61, (special issue *Sculpture & Sculptural Vessels*).

Koyama, Fujio, 1973. "Kohyama's Ceramics", Tokyo: Mitsukoshi Art Gallery.

Krauskopf, Ruth, 2005. *Palabras de tierra: Words of Clay. Ceramica Actual en Chile,* Chile: Huara Huara Taller de Ceramica.

Kuwayama, Toshimichi, 1995. *Traditional Ceramics in Shiga,* Shiga: The Museum of Modern Art.

Lurie, Samuel J. and Chang, Beatrice L., 2006. *Contemporary Japanese Ceramics: Fired with Passion,* New York: Eagle.

Lurie, Samuel J. and Gabrielle, 2009. *Love and Art,* New York: Eagle.

Mimuro, Isamu, 1996. "The Figurative Art: Slice of Earth. Yasuhisa Kohyama", in *New Japanese Ceramics* 3, Kyoto Shigaraki Iga, The Yomiuri Shinbun.

Mintz, Robert, Feinberg, Betsy and Mirviss, Joan B., 2014. *Japanese Ceramics for the Twenty-First Century: The Betsy and Robert Feinberg Collection.* Baltimore MD: The Walters Art Museum.

Museum für Kunst und Gewerbe Hamburg, 1992. *Sand und Seide. Zeitgenössische Keramik und Textilkunst aus Japan. [Yasuhisa Kohyama, Chiyoko Tanaka],* Hamburg: Museum für Kunst und Gewerbe.

Museum het Princessehof, 1992. *Kohyama and Tanaka: Contemporary Ceramics and Textile Art from Japan,* Leeuwarden: Museum het Princessehof.

Nakano, Tetuharu, 1981. "Atelier Visit: Yasuhisa Kohyama", in *Keishou,* May issue.

Nakano, Tetuharu, 1983. "Yasuhisa Kohyama Exhibition: Takashimaya Gallery Tokyo", in *Keishou*, May issue.

Osawa, Kazuto, 2014. "Slice of Clay", in *Tuchi,* Series of Japanese Origins 7 (Shinkenshinbunsha, Japan).

Pigott, Gwyn Hanssen, 2008. *Personal reflections,* London: Galerie Besson.

Shimizu, Christine and Leleu, Véronique, 2006. *Tōji: Avant-garde et tradition de la céramique japonaise,* Paris: RMN.

Stabb, Jo Ann C. and Milar, Lesley, 2012. *Retro/Prospective: 25+ Years of Art Textiles and Sculpture,* Wilton CT: browngrotta arts.

Tessier, Jean, 2000. *Voyage d'un potier français au Japon. Il était une fois un samouraï,* Paris: Maisonneuve & Larose.

Todate, Kazuko and Morse, Anne Nishimura, 2013. *Fired Earth, Woven Bamboo: Contemporary Japanese ceramics and bamboo art from the Stanley and Mary Ann Snider Collection.* Boston MA: MFA.

Watanabe, Tadashi, 1995. "Slice of Earth and Wind in Form", in *Gekkan Bijutsu,* October issue, Jitugyou no nipponsha.

Yellin, Robert, 2002. "Kohyama", Tokyo: Takashimaya Gallery.

Yoshida, Kozo, 1984. "New-classical Standardbeare Yasuhisa Kohyama", in *Geijutu Graph,* July issue, Nippon Bijutu Shuppan.

Work from the Lake Land: Ceramic Artisans of Shiga, Shiga: The Museum of Contemporary Ceramic Arts, The Shigaraki Ceramic Cultural Park.

Authors' Biographies

SUSAN JEFFERIES is an independent curator. Educated at the University of California at Berkeley, the University of Vienna, and the University of California at Davis, she had her first clay class with California Funk artist Robert Arneson. Jefferies established the modern and contemporary collections as well as a new gallery for the Gardiner Museum of Ceramic Art in Toronto, Canada, and served as its curator for ten years. Notable exhibitions include: "Jean-Pierre Larocque: Clay Sculpture and Drawings", "Bigger, Better, More: the Art of Viola Frey", and "Clay Portraits: Gertraud Möhwald". Her exhibitions of Canadian ceramics have traveled to various Asian and European countries.

MICHAEL R. CUNNINGHAM A graduate in Far Eastern Art History from the University of Chicago, Michael R. Cunningham served as curator of Japanese and Korean Art as well as chief curator of Asian Art at The Cleveland Museum of Art before retirement. During that tenure he collaborated on special exhibition projects with the Agency for Cultural Affairs (Bunka-cho), Nara National Museum, and the National Palace Museum of Korea, among other endeavors.

YOSHIAKI INUI Born in 1927, Yoshiaki Inui graduated from and became professor emeritus at Kyoto University. Known as the leading researcher in the field of contemporary ceramics in Japan, he is author of a large number of works on the history of Western art and contemporary ceramics. Yoshiaki Inui served as the former president of the Kanazawa College of Art and was former president of the Museum of Ceramic Art, Hyogo. He is currently serving as the Japanese representative to the International Academy of Ceramics.

JACK LENOR LARSEN, internationally known textile designer, author, and collector, is one of the world's foremost advocates of traditional and contemporary crafts. In addition to LongHouse Reserve, Mr. Larsen is also associated with schools and art centers worldwide. His awards include the American Craft Council Gold Medal, Cranbrook's Founders Award, The Textile Museum's Meyers Award, AIA Gold Medal, Honorary Royal Designer for Industry, and seven honorary doctorates. His designs can be found in museums and private collections around the globe.

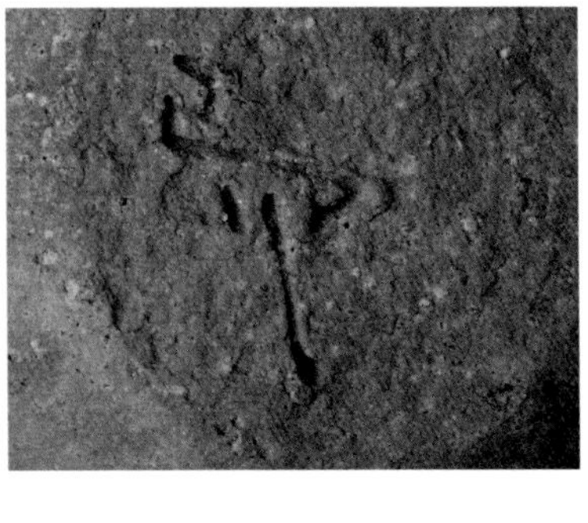